W9-CXK-144

BOAT SMART

Keeping your crew safe and well

United States Power Squadrons®

OUR MISSION
"To promote recreactional boating safetly through education and civic activities while providing fellowship for our members"

Copyright 2003, United States Power Squadrons
All rights reserved

Printed in the United States of America
United States Power Squadrons
1504 Blue Ridge Road
P. O. Box 30423
Raleigh, NC 27622
919/821-9281 • Fax: 919/836-0813
1-888-FOR-USPS (367-8777)
www.usps.org

**Contents approved by the National Association of State Boating Law Administrators
and recognized by the United States Coast Guard as acceptable
to the National Recreational Boating Safety Program**

**The Personal Watercraft Operation content of this course has been approved by the
National Association of State Boating Law Administrators as meeting requirements for a
Personal Watercraft Endorsement program.**

100803E037244

Contents

Illustrations

Introduction

There is practically no end to the enjoyment one may have around boats. To some, a boat is merely a vehicle—a tool to use for travel or work. For others, a boat is a means of entertainment. For still others, "messing about with boats is an end to itself." This course, *Boat Smart*, covers basic boating use and safety.

1 *Boat Smart* is a product of United States Power Squadrons (USPS), the world's largest private boating education organization. USPS is a group of some 60,000 men and women who share a love of boating and promoting boating safety. These men and women are all members of more than 450 individual squadrons located all over the USA. This Course is based on proven knowledge of boats and boating and is the latest iteration in a series of courses going back to 1914. Since then, more than three-million persons have taken these USPS courses.

2 USPS offers these safe boating courses:
   • *Boat Smart* (this course): an 8 hour course in the basics of safe boating.
   • *The Squadron Boating Course*: a more comprehensive 12 hour safe boating course.
   • *America's Boating Course* in partnership with the USCG-Auxiliary.
   • *Jet Smart*: a personal watercraft video course.
   • *The USPS Video Boating Course*: based on *The Squadron Boating Course*.

3 *Boat Smart* is a course for all boaters (personal watercraft operator; hunters or fishermen operating outboard utility boats; skippers of family cruisers; sailing enthusiasts). All boaters must follow the same nautical rules, regulations, and courtesies of the sea. All face the same forces of nature while boating.

4 This course is of value to all members of a boating family. USPS encourages families to attend as groups just as thousands do.

5 Qualified, enthusiastic, and experienced USPS instructors provide instruction as a civic service. There is never a charge for instruction; the only costs are those for materials, plus overhead costs such as classroom rental, shipping and handling, sales tax, etc.

6 While the content of this student manual serves as the basis for this course, it will also serve as a reference book in basic boating long after the course work is completed. The course meets the educational standards of the National Association of State Boating Law Administrators and features a proctored examination as required by many states and insurance companies. Where required, the course will provide instruction and examination for laws and regulations of state and local authorities in the areas where the course is taught.

7 USPS believes that the more educated a boater becomes, the more likely that boater will be a safe boater. *Boat Smart* is the beginning of a boating education. USPS encourages students to follow this brief and basic course with additional boating education offered to members of the United States Power Squadrons. Your instructors can give you information about these advanced courses as well as membership in USPS.

8 The USPS Mission Statement
To promote recreational boating safety through education and civic activities while providing fellowship for our members.

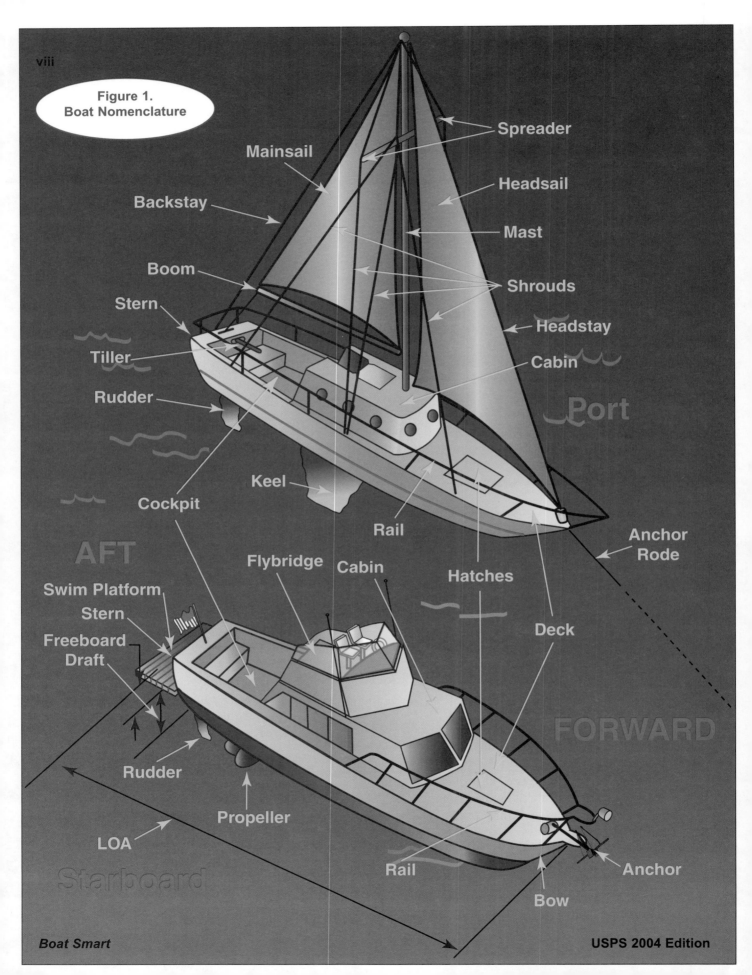

Figure 1.
Boat Nomenclature

Mainsail

Spreader

Headsail

Backstay

Mast

Boom

Shrouds

Stern

Headstay

Tiller

Cabin

Rudder

Port

Cockpit

Keel

Rail

Anchor
Rode

AFT

Flybridge   Cabin

Hatches

Swim Platform

Stern

Deck

Freeboard
Draft

Rudder

Propeller

Rail

LOA

FORWARD

Starboard

Anchor

Bow

Boat Smart

USPS 2004 Edition

1

Getting Started

We go boating for fun . . . it is always more fun to be confident and know what to do and when to do it. When you can do that consistently, both you, your crew, and your guests will be safer and have more fun.

Boat Terms and Types

1 We begin by describing a few of the more common parts of boats in nautical terms. Why? Because in an emergency—or when fast action is required—there will be no time for definitions or clarifications. "Throw me a line" is not about jokes. It is about needing a rope very quickly. Following this will be brief descriptions of various common boat types. Note that there is an Appendix A to this book that is a glossary. The terms you see in *italics* appear in detail there.

Terms

2 Take a close look at the two boats on the facing page. One is a sailboat and the other a powerboat. They're about the same size, but have dramatically different looks and parts. Yet on each the basic structure is the *hull*. On each, the most *forward* end is the *bow*, while the *aft* or *after* end is the *stern*. A *transom* is that portion of the hull at the stern that is at right angles to the centerline of each boat. The upper edge of the hull is the *gunwale* which is pronounced "gun'l."

> Compare the names of the various parts of each of these two boats.

3 The *deck* covers the hull, and the *bilge* is the lowest part of the interior of the hull, under the *sole* which is the floor of a cockpit or interior cabin. A *cabin* is an enclosed living space on a boat; a *cuddy* is a small cabin without full headroom. The *cockpit* is a sunken space below the gunwale line.

4 A *flybridge* is an elevated steering position on a powerboat. *Berths* are sleeping accommodations on a boat. A *head* is a marine toilet (and its compartment). A *galley* is a nautical kitchen.

5 A boat can be steered with a *rudder*, a moveable underwater blade attached to a *rudder post* and moved with a lever called a *tiller* or a cable or hydraulic arrangement connected to a wheel. Whether a tiller or a wheel, the steering mechanism and its location in the boat are referred to as the *helm*.

6 *Forward* is toward the *bow*, or front; aft is toward the back, or stern. The right side of the boat and the direction to the right are *starboard*, while the left side and the direction to the left are *port*.

7 *Length overall* (LOA) is the length of the hull, excluding any attachments. *Beam* is the maximum width of the hull. *Draft* is how deeply the hull penetrates the water. *Freeboard* is the distance from the water to the lowest point of a boat where water could come aboard.

8 *Spars* are poles that support sails. A *mast* is a vertical spar on which sails are set and on powerboats where flags and burgees may be flown. A *boom* is a horizontal spar supporting the bottom edge of a sail.

9 A *mainsail* is a boat's principal sail. A *head-*

sail is any sail flown forward of the mainmast. A *jib* is a common headsail, usually smaller than the big-bellied *spinnaker.*

10 *Shrouds* are lines that support a mast side-to-side, and are attached to the sides of the hull through *chain plates. Stays* are lines that support a mast *fore* and aft. A *forestay* runs from the top of the mast forward to the bow; a *backstay* runs from the mast to the stern. Together, shrouds and stays that serve to support spars are called *standing rigging.*

11 Lines used to raise, set, and *trim* sails are collectively referred to as *running rigging.* There are many specialized names for these and other features, but the two main types of running rigging are *halyards*, used to lift sails, flags, etc., to the top of the mast, and *sheets*, used to control sails and booms.

Construction Materials

12 There is no such thing as an ideal boat-building material. Wood served well for hundreds of years; it is strong, can be beautiful, is relatively easy to work with and to repair. Wooden boats require a large amount of maintenance. Nevertheless, their good points are so many that many boaters would have no other material.

13 Most boats used for recreation today are constructed of glass-reinforced plastic, or fiberglass. Fiberglass boats are strong, reasonably light weight, available at reasonable cost, and require a minimum of maintenance. Their availability has had much to do with the great popularity of recreational boating today. Other materials used in boat construction include aluminum, steel, ferrocement, and neoprene-coated fabrics.

Boat Types

14 The number of styles, designs, models, and sizes of boats can be bewildering to a person shopping for a first boat. Choosing the right boat is the first step in enjoying boating. The best boat is almost always a compromise of some sort or another.

Figure 2.
Small Boats . . .Utility (Top),
Inflatable (Center),
and Runabout (Bottom).

15 **Utility boats** include a myriad of regional types—*dinghies*, rowboats, skiffs, flatties, sneak boats, bass boats, etc.— all purpose-designed to meet specific needs and conditions. These boats were usually designed originally to be rowed or paddled, but may be powered by *outboard* motors or sails. They are usually very basic in their construction, but may be very sophisticated, with features and design optimized for a specific application.

16 **Inflatables** can also be used as utility boats, especially as *tenders* for larger craft because

they can bounce off another boat's hull without damage. They are stable in the water, and can be powered by small outboard motors.

17 **Runabouts** range from small outboard-powered boats to large ocean racers with multiple engines. They are "sporty" boats usually lacking cooking, sleeping, and head facilities, although some runabouts have some or all of these features.

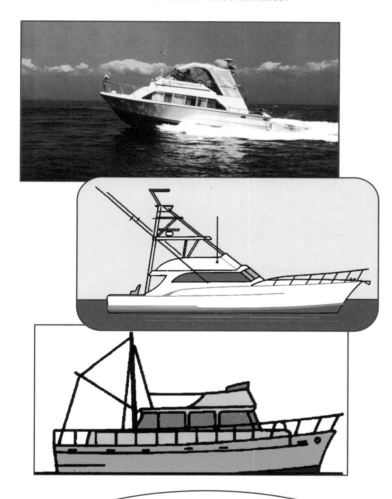

Figure 3.
Cruiser for Lakes and Inland Waters (Top),
Sportfisher for Offshore Sport (Center),
and Trawler for Comfort (Bottom)

18 **Cruisers** are more *seaworthy* and offer more accommodations. They range from twenty-foot weekenders to yachts over one hundred feet long. Cruisers have berths, heads, and galleys. Large cruisers often rival luxury homes.

19 **Sportfishermen** are fast, high-powered cruisers with open aft cockpits suited for fishing.

20 **Trawlers** are cruisers that emphasize comfort and stability rather than speed, usually capable of long-range cruising.

Figure 4.
Houseboat (Top)
Pontoon Boat (Below)

21 **Houseboats** offer spacious living quarters at deck level and may have a flying bridge and sun deck above the *deckhouse*. Most houseboats should not ordinarily be taken into exposed waters; their hull designs and *superstructures* with large expanses of windows make them vulnerable to storm action and high *seas*.

22 **Pontoon boats** originated as wooden rafts set on steel drums. Now these boats are often sophisticated and fast fiberglass, aluminum, or steel boats with many amenities. They are very popular on sheltered waters.

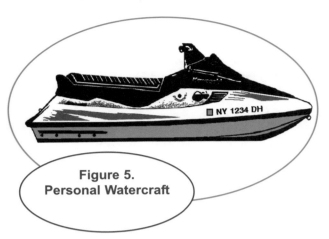

Figure 5.
Personal Watercraft

23 **Personal watercraft (PWC)** are small one-to-three passenger boats which the operator and passenger(s) straddle (as a motorcycle) or stand or kneel on. PWCs are powered by enclosed water jet pumps since exposed propellers would be dangerous.

24 **Sailboats** are made in many sizes and styles from very small *day sailers* to very large cruising sailboats with *auxiliary* power and luxurious accommodations. The more common configurations of sailboats are the catboat, sloop, cutter, ketch, and yawl. Larger ocean-cruising sailboats are often motor-sailers which combine the better features of sail and power boats.

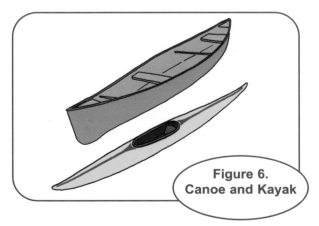

Figure 6.
Canoe and Kayak

25 **Canoes and Kayaks** are popular in inland waters. Both are usually propelled by paddles, although canoes may be equipped with small outboard motors. Both craft are relatively unstable, but are correspondingly agile. Knowledge, skill, and experience are neces-

sary for their safe use, but can take you to into waterways unavailable to other types of boat.

Catboat
Mast near bow, no headsail

Sloop
Single mast about 40% aft of bow with headsail and mainsail

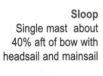

Cutter
Single mast nearer midship with two headsails and mainsail

Ketch
Two masts with the aftermast forward of the rudder post

Yawl
Two masts with the aftermast aft of the rudder post

Figure 7. Sailboats

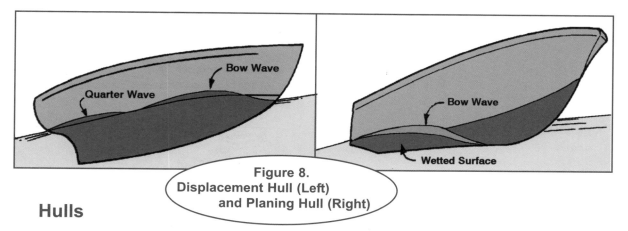

Figure 8.
Displacement Hull (Left)
and Planing Hull (Right)

Hulls

26 There are two basic types of hull, *displacement* and *planing*. Each is significantly different from the other.

27 **Displacement Hulls.** Lower a boat into the water and some of the water must move out of the way to accommodate the boat. If you could weigh that displaced water, you would find it equals the weight of the boat. That weight is the boat's *displacement*.

28 A displacement hull moves through the water by pushing the water aside. Vessels with displacement hulls are limited to slower speeds than those with planing hulls. The theoretical speed of a displacement hull is related to the waterline length—the longer the waterline, the greater the potential hull speed. Most large cruisers, (including trawlers), and most sailboats are displacement boats.

29 **Planing Hulls** operate as displacement hulls at rest or slow speeds, but climb towards the surface of the water as they move faster. They skim along at high speed, riding almost on top of the water rather than pushing it aside. Runabouts, most smaller cruisers, sportfishermen, personal watercraft, and a few small sailboats are examples of planing vessels.

30 Many boats combine features of both displacement and planing hull designs. They are capable of performing effectively at low speed as displacement hulls and at high speed when planing. These are often referred to as semi-displacement hulls.

31 **Bottom Shapes.** The bottom of a boat may be one of three basic shapes—round, flat, or vee. Round bottom boats are displacement hulls, offering a slow but comfortable ride through the water. However, they tend to roll and can be unstable.

32 Flat bottom boats are the basic planing hull. They ride roughly and tend to pound in choppy water, but are relatively stable. They are usually inexpensive to build.

33 Boats with deep-vee bottoms are variants of planing hulls. They offer good stability and less pounding in rough water than others.

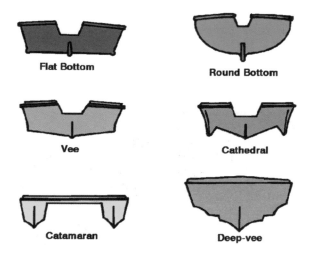

Figure 9. Boat Bottom Shapes

34 Boat hulls may be combinations of types. They may be one type forward, gradually changing to another type toward the stern in an attempt to balance advantages and drawbacks to provide hull performance that buyers will like. Or they may be arranged as two or three hull shapes joined together as a *catamaran*, *trimaran*, or other variant.

35 ## Factors Affecting Seaworthiness
Three important features of a boat affect its seaworthiness and safety:
- size
- design
- construction materials.

The size and design play a large part in its buoyancy and stability. The stronger the construction materials, the safer and more seaworthy it will be.

Propulsion Systems

36 There are two basic types of boat power plants: *outboard* motors and *inboard* engines.

37 **Outboard** motors are mounted on the transom or special brackets on the transom. They move the boat with a propeller. The motor and its lower unit pivot to steer the boat. Usually lighter in weight than inboard engines, they do not take up space inside the boat. Outboards are detachable from the boat, making servicing and replacement easy and less expensive than servicing and replacing inboard motors.

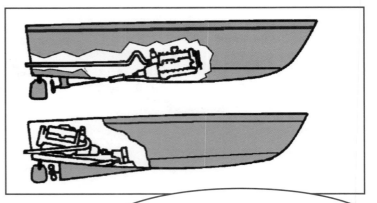

Figure 11. Boats with Inboard Engines. Straight Shaft Drive (Top) Vee-Drive (Bottom)

38 **Inboard** engines are mounted inside the boat hull. They transmit power from the engine to a propeller or water jet pump through a *shaft*. To turn a propeller, the shaft passes through a special fitting in the hull that allows it to rotate while keeping out most of the water. The small amount of water that does enter actually serves to lubricate the fitting. (The fitting should be checked frequently to ensure that there is no excess leakage, as this is a major cause of boats sinking at the pier.)

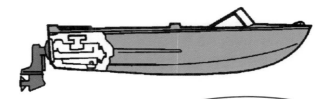

Figure 12. Boat with Stern Drive (I/O)

39 **Stern drive** (often called inboard/outboard or *I/O*) has features of both inboards and outboards. Stern drives operate with an inboard engine, but the drive shaft exits through a special fitting in the transom, through a series of gears, shafts, and couplings, to a lower unit similar to that of an outboard motor. Turning the lower unit steers the boat.

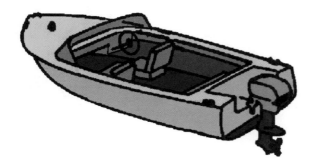

Figure 10. Boat with Outboard Motor

40 Most powerboats are propelled by a propeller,

sometimes called a *screw*. These are multi-bladed rotating wheels that draw in water from *ahead* and push it out astern. Twin-screw boats have two engines and two propellers.

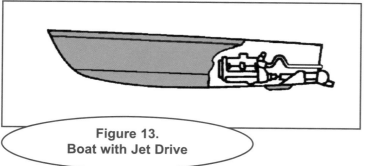

**Figure 13.
Boat with Jet Drive**

41 **Jet drives** have no external propeller. The engine drives a water pump, which forces large quantities of water under high pressure through an external jet. The force of the water pushes the boat through the water. You steer the boat by moving the jet from side to side. This system is used in Personal Watercraft. Jet boats are particularly useful in certain applications such as shallow, rocky rivers where a traditional propeller and rudder arrangement would be easily damaged.

Select the Right Boat

42 When shopping for a boat, some planning is in order. Here are some of the questions you should address before visiting a showroom or boat yard:

- What type and style will best serve your planned use of the boat?
- Will you be boating in open seas, coastal waters, or more protected lakes and rivers?
- How large a boat do you need for the number of people who will be accompanying you?
- Have you considered not only initial expense but operational, maintenance, and storage expenses?

Know What You Buy

43 Obtain advice from knowledgeable persons you trust about brands and types of boats that interest you. Check with the USCG Customer Infoline to determine if there have been consumer complaints or safety recalls on a boat that catches your eye. Boaters in the United States, including Alaska, Hawaii, Puerto Rico, and the Virgin Islands, may call 1-800-368-5647 to reach Infoline. (Alternate numbers are 1-800-869-0815 for the hearing impaired and 1-212-267-2100 in the Washington DC area.) Hours are 8:00 A.M. to 4:00 P.M. Eastern Standard Time, Monday through Friday, except on federal holidays.

Finding Your Way

44 Would you start a long cross-country automobile trip without first consulting a road map? Out there on the highway there are many signs to help you follow the roads. But, on the water, there are few defined roads and signposts. On the water you may think you have endless options as to where you can go. The problem is that hazards you cannot see often lurk just beneath the surface. Coastline features often lack crisp definition to help determine your location. On the water you need the marine equivalent of highway road maps. These are called *charts*. You should not leave port without the correct chart of your area.

Charts

45 Charts are different from maps. Maps show the general direction of roads plus the general location of other features. That's not good enough for marine charts. Marine charts emphasize features affecting accurate navigation. These include:

- Expected depths
- Shipping lanes and hazards
- Aids to navigation
- Local features and regulations

As a skipper, it is your responsibility to have up-to-date charts aboard your boat of the areas where you operate. Become thoroughly familiar with them and what they show you.

46 Charts show where you can—and cannot—safely operate your boat. A small portion of the chart of the area around Point Judith, RI appears in Figure 15. The land areas are brown. The areas of deeper water are white. Shallow water is blue with depths shown as numbers. Aids to navigation appear (see Chapter 3) as well as shore features useful for determining your location while on the water. At the left side of the chart is the scale for latitude. The line along the bottom of this portion of the chart is 41°20rNorth Latitude. The vertical black line passing through the right corner of the Marsh and up through Wakefield is 71°30rWest Longitude. The heavy black lines on the chart are plots of courses and bearings with times, true course, speeds and direction added. The circled position showing 0800 at the Harbor of Refuge is at 41°21.9rN Latitude and 71°31.9rW Longitude.

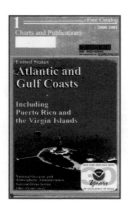

**Figure 14
Chart Catalog.
(Free from NOAA
and Authorized
Dealers.)**

47 The National Oceanic and Atmospheric Administration (NOAA), publishes coastal and offshore charts (more than 1,000). The Army Corps of Engineers publishes charts of the Great Lakes. Charts are supplied in several scales (1:1,500 to 1:600,000). A 1:1,500 chart shows much greater detail than the 1:600,000 chart. You can find your location on a chart—when you know what to look for. Free catalogs of all NOAA charts are available from NOAA and authorized dealers. The catalog for the Atlantic and Gulf Coasts

is shown in Figure 14. This is one of four NOAA chart catalogs

Piloting

48 The art and science of finding your way on the water with the help of visible marks is called *piloting*. An overview of piloting principles and techniques is part of the USPS course *Chart Smart*. Greater detail appears in the USPS member courses *Piloting* and *Advanced Piloting*.

49 Charts are used to plan safe boat trips from one point to another. These charts help boaters avoid hazards, busy shipping lanes and restricted areas. From a carefully plotted course on a chart you can know what course to steer, when to make necessary turns and the distance. By applying speed, you can determine your time in transit and when you should be at specific points along the way. Piloting by compass direction, time and speed is called *dead reckoning*. Skilled pilots have used this method for centuries, but there are other factors to consider—wind, current and compass error can affect the accuracy of the plotted course.

Electronic Navigation

50 Modern boaters have navigation tools unavailable just a few short years ago. First came Loran and now GPS *(Global Positioning System)*. GPS uses an array of satellites to provide precise three-dimensional positioning anyplace on Earth. Modern GPS receivers are marvels of reliable (but not infallible) engineering requiring practice to master. GPS tells you where you are in terms of latitude, longitude and altitude. (Altitude is of little value to boaters.) Use this to plot your location on some reference chart. If you have the proper electronic instruments on the boat an electronic chart plotter does this for you. You use these positions to determine your progress on your predetermined course and dead reckoning. When used properly, GPS provides a navigation tool of uncanny accuracy plus convenience.

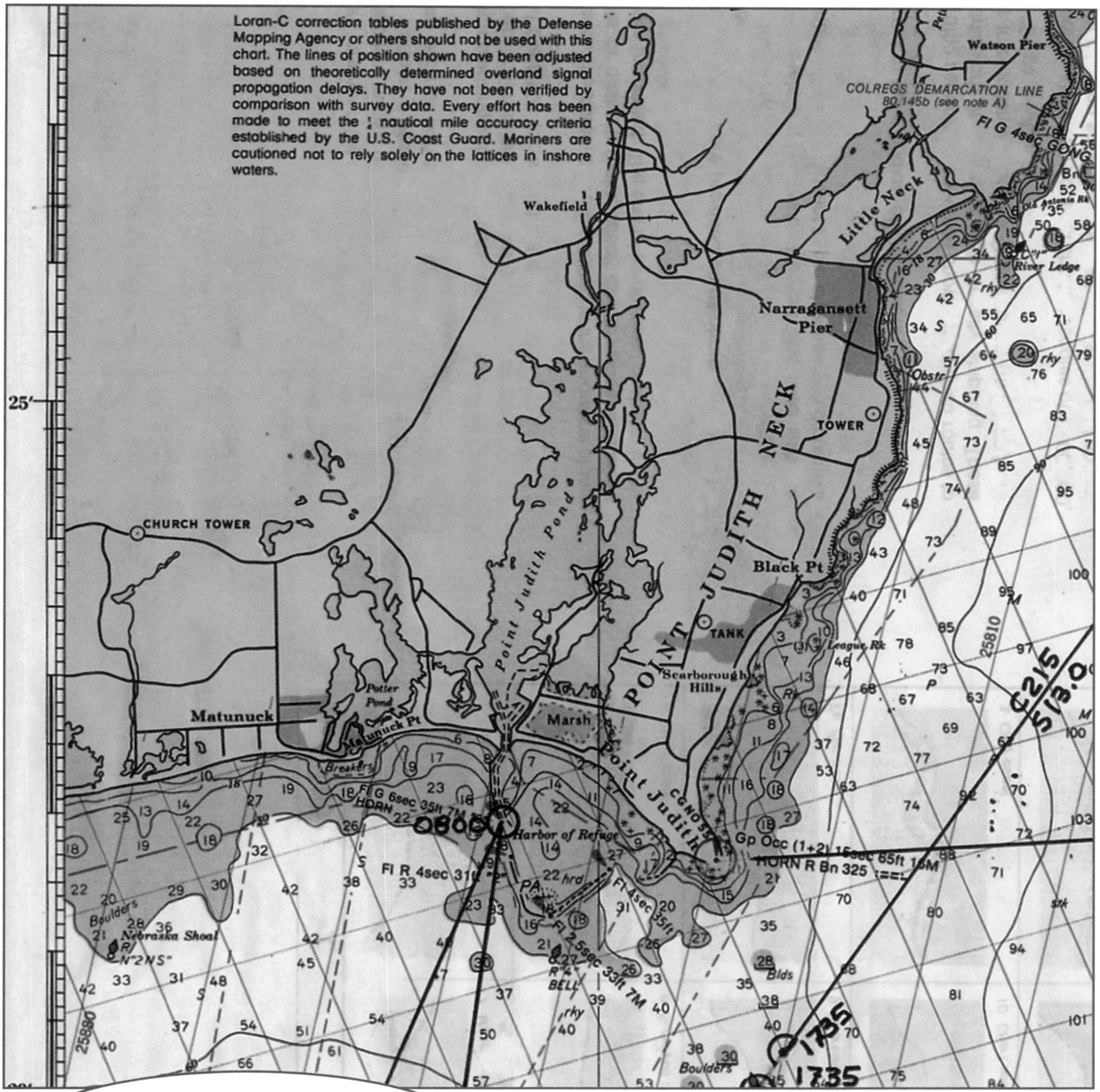
Loran-C correction tables published by the Defense Mapping Agency or others should not be used with this chart. The lines of position shown have been adjusted based on theoretically determined overland signal propagation delays. They have not been verified by comparison with survey data. Every effort has been made to meet the ¼ nautical mile accuracy criteria established by the U.S. Coast Guard. Mariners are cautioned not to rely solely on the lattices in inshore waters.
Wakefield
Watson Pier
COLREGS DEMARCATION LINE
80.145b (see note A)
Fl G 4sec GONG
Little Neck
River Ledge
Narragansett Pier
Obstr
TOWER
POINT JUDITH NECK
Point Judith Pond
CHURCH TOWER
Black Pt
TANK
League Rk
Scarborough Hills
Potter Pond
Matunuck
Matunuck Pt
Marsh
Breakers
Fl G 6sec 35ft 7M HORN
0800
Harbor of Refuge
Point Judith
Gp Occ (1+2) 15sec 65ft 16M
HORN R Bn 325
Fl R 4sec 31ft
Fl 4sec 35ft
Fl 2.5sec 33ft 7M
BELL
Boulders
Nebraska Shoal
C215
S13.0
1735
25'

Figure 15
A Portion of a Nautical Chart

51 By comparing your current position with that of just one second ago, GPS tells you the direction you are heading and at what speed you are travelling. GPS can compare your position to one previously stored in the unit to give you bearing and distance from where you were—as well as where you plan to be. You store these locations in the unit's memory and they are called *waypoints.*

52 GPS allows a piloting method called *way-point navigation*. You travel along predetermined straight-line segments (called *legs*) from one waypoint to the next. Obviously, these waypoints must be pre-selected and stored in the GPS by latitude/longitude coordinates and given an identifying name (number). A current chart is an absolute necessity so the chosen path is free of hazards and is safe to travel. Although GPS is a marvelous convenience, no boater should ever rely on a single source for navigation information. Always plot your course progress on a chart and watch for all other indications of location. USPS offers the *GPS Seminar* program. Watch for it in your area. Remember that you are navigating blindly if you do not have the current charts to use with GPS. Just as you wouldn't start a long cross-country automobile trip without consulting road maps, you shouldn't leave port without appropriate marine *charts*. Charts differ from maps by emphasizing features of the water that are of interest to mariners. These features include: expected depths, location of aids to navigation, obstructions, etc. You should have charts of the area where you are boating onboard, and you should be thoroughly familiar with them and what they mean.

Operator Responsibilities

53 A boat operator (skipper) is responsible for the safety of everyone aboard and for operating the boat in a safe and respectful manner. This includes minimizing engine noise and boat speed in congested or restricted waters. Skippers are legally responsible for these activities as well as any reckless or negligent boat operation.

Homeland Security Measures

54 Boaters need to be aware of rules and guidelines regarding homeland security measures. Following are steps boaters can take to protect our country and are a direct result of the terrorist attacks of 11 September 2001.

Restricted Areas:
- Keep your distance from all military, cruise line, and commercial shipping vessels.
- Proceed at a no-wake speed when within a Protection Zone (500 yards from a U.S. naval vessel).
- As a non-military vessel, do not come within 100 yards of a U.S. naval vessel, underway or moored, unless authorized by an official Coast Guard or Navy patrol.
- Understand that a violation of the Naval Vessel Protection Zone is a felony offense and is punishable by up to six years imprisonment and/or up to a $250,000 fine.
- Observe and avoid all security zones, commercial port operation areas, and restricted areas near: • Dams • Power Plants • Naval Shipyards • Dry Docks
- Do not stop or anchor beneath bridges or in channels.
- Keep your boat locked when not aboard even when temporarily docked at yacht clubs, restaurants, marinas, etc.
- When storing your boat, disable the engine. If it is on a trailer, immobilize it so it cannot be moved.
- Keep a sharp eye out for anything that looks peculiar or out of the ordinary and report it to the Coast Guard or port/marine security.
- When boating within a foreign country, be sure to check in with the U.S. Customs Service and/or Immigration and Naturalization Service. Know the rules before you go abroad so there are no unpleasant surprises when you begin your return home.

Restricted Areas and Security Zones shown on Charts

55 Restricted Areas are shown on navigational charts with a broken line around the perimeter of the area or zone. Examples where these areas may be found on charts are military bases, naval docking facilities, shipyards servicing military vessels, power

plants, bridges, and other areas that have been so designated. At the request of the Captain of the Port, or District Commander, these areas may also be designated a Security Zones and may be highlighted in a magenta color, so they standout better in warning the public to stay clear. Non-authorized vessels without specific permission to enter are instructed to stay out of these marked areas. Armed military, harbor police, or civilian authorities will likely confront violators.

Boat Handling

54 Learning to operate a boat properly, like learning to drive an automobile, comes with experience. You can learn the principles of boat handling before going on the water, but there is no substitute for hands-on experience in your own boat.

Fueling

55 Gasoline vapors are heavier than air and will settle into the bilge of a boat. The vapors are highly explosive when mixed with air. (Diesel fuel, while still a hazard, is less dangerous than gasoline.) Prevent gasoline, either liquid or vapor, from getting into your bilge. If your boat has a blower, operate it until you are sure there are no more fumes before you start the engine. Never start the engine until you have sniffed for fuel vapors in the engine and fuel tank compartments.

56 Check the condition of your tanks, hoses, and fuel line connections several times during the season. Look for corrosion, loose fittings, and soft, cracked or brittle hoses. If you have any doubts, replace the questionable parts immediately. This is especially true of older or used boats with an unknown maintenance history. All gasoline fuels now contain alcohol and alcohol will deteriorate synthetic fuel hoses and gaskets. Make sure your gasoline-powered boat has alcohol-resistant fuel-system components.

57 Mark your deck filler caps for fuel (gasoline or diesel), water, and waste. People have put diesel fuel into gasoline tanks, and gasoline into water tanks, waste holding tanks, and fishing rod holders.

58 **Fueling Checklists.** Develop a consistent routine when fueling your boat by following these fueling checklists:

59 **Before-Fueling Checklist**
- Fuel in daylight, if possible.
- Tie your boat securely to the fuel dock.
- Extinguish all flames, such as cigarettes, pipes, lamps, galley stoves.
- Shut off engines and any electrical equipment that might create a spark, including blowers and radios.
- Close all windows, ports, doors, hatches.
- Have an operable fire extinguisher close by.
- Have crew and passengers not needed for fueling go ashore.

60 **While-Fueling Checklist**
- Take portable tanks out of the boat and fill them on the dock.
  Warning! Never fill a portable fuel tank while it is on the non-metallic bed of a pickup truck. Static electricity will build up and ignite the fuel. Remove the tank from the truck and refill it on the ground.
- Keep the pump nozzle in constant metal-to-metal contact with the filler pipe to eliminate the chance of static electricity causing a spark and igniting fuel vapor.
- Estimate the amount of fuel needed and listen to the sound of the entering fuel. With experience you will be able to tell when the tank is nearly full.

61 **After-Fueling Checklist
(Before Starting Your Engines)**

- Close fuel filler pipe openings.
- Wipe up any spillage. Leave the wipers ashore.
- Open all closed compartments and turn on the bilge blower.
- Sniff in the tank and engine compartments for gasoline vapors.
- Start your engines and leave the dock as soon as you are sure there is no hazard. It is not courteous or safe to linger.

Preparing to Cast Off

62 Do not wait for emergencies to happen. Make sure your boat is ready before you get under way, preferably using a checklist.

63 **Check the Weather Forecast.** Get an up-to-date forecast for the area where you plan to cruise. The current National Weather Service forecasts are available on your *VHF* marine radio. These forecasts are updated several times a day and more often when severe weather develops. If the forecast predicts high waves or high winds, stay ashore and wait for a better day. Never venture out into conditions that could be beyond the scope of your ability and the capabilities of your boat.

64 **Know Local Hazards.** As part of your preparation, learn whether there are dams and locks or whitewater areas where you will be boating. Get local advice and be alert if boating near known hazards. Always obtain charts of lakes and rivers where you go boating.

65 **File a Float Plan.** If you are going for just a few hours on your boat, let someone know where you plan to be and when you expect to return. If you plan a longer cruise, leave a copy of a written *float plan* with your marina, yacht club, or friend. A float plan includes a description of your boat, who is on board, a description of the safety equipment you are carrying, where you expect to be, and when you expect to be there. Instruct the person holding the float plan to notify the Coast Guard or other appropriate agency if you do not return within a reasonable time after your scheduled arrival (taking into account weather, etc.). When you arrive at your destination, or if your plans change, notify the person holding your float plan to avoid unnecessary worry and possible waste of search and rescue resources. There is no special or official form that you must use for a float plan, though you may find convenient pre-printed ones available in boating supply stores and catalogues. Appendix E of this manual is a float plan form.

66 **Checklists** are valuable tools to help you remember things. Having lists individualized for your own boat, where you sail it, and the use to which you put it can help you prevent both inconvenience and potential danger. Below are examples of equipment and systems checklists you can use as the basis for making lists for your boat. You will also find some additional equipment suggestions grouped by boat size in Chapter 2 (What's Needed) of this manual.

67 **Equipment Checklist**
- Personal papers; operator's certificate or license on board.
- Ship's papers; registration or documentation certificate, radio license posted (if required).
- An FCC Radio License is not required for a boat with a marine radiotelephone operating in U.S. waters. A recreational vessel when traveling in foreign waters with a radio telephone onboard or communicating with a foreign station from U.S. waters must have a posted current ship radio license.
- Life jacket suitable for each person on board, available, in good condition.
- Throwable flotation aid.
- Fire extinguishers conveniently placed, fully charged, in good condition.
- Visual distress signals with current expiration dates.

- Horn working.
- Bell (if required) on board.
- Anchor and anchor line appropriate to area, depth, conditions.
- Compass properly adjusted.
- Charts for the area, up to date.
- Navigation tools.
- Boat hook.
- Mooring lines and fenders in good condition.
- Paddles or oars.
- Tool kit and spare parts (including light bulbs, fuses).

68 **Vessel Systems Checklist**

- Bilge free of fuel vapors and excess water.
- Fuel supply full.
- Fuel system free of leaks.
- Engine oil and transmission fluid levels correct.
- Battery fully charged, fluid level full.
- Electronic gear in good condition.
- Engine drive belts tight, in good condition.
- All navigation lights working.
- Steering and shift mechanisms in good condition.
- Outboard motor mountings tight(if appropriate).
- Grab rails, life-lines in good condition.

69 **Load Gear and Passengers Properly.** Small boats can be unstable, and falls are always a risk. Always step into a boat—never jump—and hold onto something whenever possible. Step into the center of small boats, never on the gunwale (the upper edge of a boat).

70 Be sure of your footing and be especially careful of wet surfaces. Always load gear aboard from the pier and never try to carry heavy or bulky things aboard in your arms.

71 Keep people off the *foredeck*, gunwales, seat backs, and transom of small boats. Passengers should sit in the seats provided. Trim the boat so that it rides evenly in the water. Remember that weight carried high in a boat can make it unstable. Keep heavy weights (including people) low. Secure all loose gear. Overloading is a major cause of boating accidents. Never overload your boat or use a motor larger than is recommended. All single hull boats under 20 feet (except personal watercraft) have a Coast Guard Maximum Capacities Label advising you of the maximum combined weight of persons, motor and gear permitted for your boat.

72 **Life Jackets.** Assign a life jacket [personal flotation device (PFD), life preserver] to each person on board. Have them put it on and adjust it to fit. The best insurance is to wear a life jacket at all times. (See additional details in Chapter 3 on USCG PFD regulations effective 23 Dec 2002 for children.)

73 **Start and Warm the Engines.** Remember the admonition given previously about fueling: Never start your engines until you are sure the engine and fuel compartments are free of gasoline vapors. Use the bilge blower for at least five minutes, raise the engine hatch and use your nose.

74 With engine(s) running, make sure that cooling water is flowing through the system. Check gauges and indicator lights to insure they are working and reading properly. With an outboard motor, you should see water flowing out of the port on the engines. With an inboard (or I/O) you should see water vapor coming out of the exhaust.

75 **Train an Alternate Skipper.** At least one other person aboard should be able to start and stop the engines (or raise, set, and lower the sails) and use the radio in case of an emergency. Ideally, an alternate skipper should also be able to anchor the boat or take the helm and return it to your mooring.

76 **Boat Preventive Maintenance.**
A safe boater maintains the boat, constantly checking and inspecting for potential
problems. This includes checking all
through-hull fittings, engines and engine-
related equipment, oil and fuel levels, and
electrical systems. A problem resolved at
the dock is less hassle than one that must
be repaired while on the water. Consider
the difference between fixing something
while tied up at the dock versus trying to
do the job in heavy winds or seas, or while
drifting into dangerous waters. Here the
adage, "An ounce of prevention is worth a
pound of cure," is worth heeding.

Getting Under Way

77 The exciting moment has arrived, but before
you actually get underway, always observe
proper procedures.

78 **Passenger Communication.** As the
skipper you are obliged to inform everyone
onboard about safety matters including:

- Information on the location and proper use
of life jackets (PFDs), fire extinguishers,
and visual distress equipment.

- Discussing the rules about discharging
waste overboard, emergency procedures, and basic operation of the marine
radio (if installed), and the location of
the first-aid kit.

- Any other information of which you are
aware, based on the operating area and
the weather and/or water conditions you
may encounter.

79 **Plan Your Departure.** Before *casting off*
dock lines, take a good look around your
immediate surroundings and plan what you
are going to do. Are there other boats in the
vicinity? What is the direction of the wind
and *current*? How do you plan to deal with
it? Tell the others on board what you plan to
do and what you expect to happen, and
assign them clear duties within their abilities. Then ask yourself what could possibly

go wrong. What would you do about it if
(when) that happens?

80 **Departure Checklist**
- Disconnect all utility lines such as power
cords and water lines.
- Take in all dock lines and fenders (protective devices used between the boat and
other objects) except for those you will
use in leaving the dock.
- Instruct passengers and crew to keep
hands, arms, etc., inside the boat.
- Sound proper whistle (horn) signals.
- After clearing the dock area, take in all
lines and fenders and keep them clear
of the propeller.
- Keep a lookout at all times for other boats,
persons, and objects in the water.
- Keep a watch for low overhead wires.
- Proceed slowly whenever leaving or
returning to a dock.
- Use just enough power to maintain control.

81 **Leaving the Pier.** Boats steer differently
than cars. Cars steer from the front—boats
steer from the rear. In the middle of a lake
or in the ocean this difference makes no
difference at all. But when close to a pier
or another boat, it makes all the difference
in the world. A boat turns by moving the
stern to one side or the other until the bow
points in the desired direction. If you are
close to a person in the water, a piling, a
pier, or another boat, you should avoid
turning the rudder in a direction that will
cause the stern to run over the person in
the water or cause the stern to hit something close.

82 Wind and current move a boat around in a
way seldom experienced by cars on the
road. Even simple maneuvers require
thought. Plan ahead. Don't put yourself into
a position from which you cannot easily
recover should something go wrong. Every
situation is unique. No single maneuver

works all the time. Still, there are general principles that can be useful guides.

83 Some boats are sensitive to the effects of wind; others are more affected by current. Some boats are nimble, and respond quickly to the helm and throttle; others are more stodgy (slow to take a new *course*), or once on it, slow to depart from it. Experience will tell you the type of boat you have. In general, planing hulls are affected little by current when up to cruising speed.

84 Houseboats and other vessels with large structures and shallow draft are affected greatly by wind. Boats with deep draft or large *keels* (boats with lots of surface area underwater) can be affected more by current than by wind. Sailboats are affected by both current and wind. Boats with small rudders do not maneuver at low speed as well as those with large rudders. At anchor, a boat's response to wind and current is often unpredictable. Always allow for ample swinging room when anchoring.

85 The secret of being a good seaman lies in knowing how all these factors work on your boat. You can then turn them to your advantage to help you make the maneuver you want to make. For example, suppose you want to take your boat away from the *pier*. If the wind is blowing away from the pier, all you need to do is cast off the lines and let the wind carry you away until it is safe to move ahead. If the wind is from ahead, you can push the bow away from the pier and make a slow and gradual turn until your stern is clear of the pier. Remember—the stern controls the steering of the boat. With wind or current from *astern*, you can usually push the stern away and back the boat away enough to clear the pier.

86 With wind or current on the pier, use an *after bow spring line*—a dock line leading aft from a boat's bow to the pier. With the spring line fastened and fenders protecting the boat, move slowly forward against the spring line and turn the rudder to move the stern away

from the pier. The spring line will hold the bow while the engine moves the stern out. When the boat is at an approximately 45-degree angle with the pier, release the spring line and back away.

While Underway

87 Responsible boat operation requires observance of rules and knowing how to handle the boat properly.

88 **Boat's Wake.** A wake is a trail of large waves created by a moving boat. Take precautions to protect your boat by using proper mooring lines, adequate fenders, etc. A wake from a passing boat can easily snap lines and overwhelm fenders. *You* are responsible for injuries or damage to property caused by the wake of your boat.

89 Observe **NO WAKE** signs. Remember, too, that some boats make more of a wake at 5 mph than they do at 25 mph, so even if the sign specifies a 5 MPH limit slow down so you produce no wake, even if that means operating at idle speed.

90 You will find NO WAKE zones at:
- launching ramps.
- fuel docks.
- marinas.
- anchored, beached or rafted boats.
- swimming beaches.
- sailing regattas, power boat races.
- bridges, locks, canals or narrow passages.
- any other areas designated by appropriate authorities as "NO WAKE" areas.

91 **Turning.** High speed turns can lead to a loss of control. People can be thrown overboard, and the boat can overturn (*capsize*). Heavy seas or wakes increase the chance of these accidents happening. Always turn at a slow, controllable speed

92 **Backing.** Boats are made to move forward, not backward. The shape of the stern is often flat and may be cut away for an outboard motor. Water can pile up against the transom or even come into the boat. Always back slowly. Learn how your boat reacts to backing. Some boats, especially those with a single screw, will not back in a straight line, but veer off to one side (usually to port).

93 **Waves.** Waves can affect both the forward movement of the boat and its steering. Seas striking forward of amidships tend to decrease speed through the water. Waves coming up astern can increase speed in short bursts.

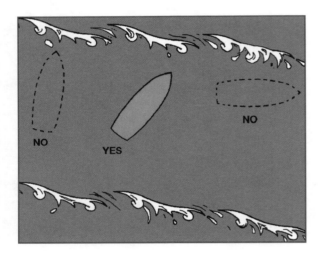

Figure 16. Boat Running Into Waves.

94 Waves will cause a boat to turn broadside into the trough between the waves. The helmsman must continually adjust the throttle and rudder to stay on course.

95 **Running into waves** can be fatiguing for the crew and hard on the boat and its equipment. You can ease the shock on both boat and crew by slowing down and taking the waves at an angle to the bow, not head-on. Experimentation will determine the best angle for your hull, which will vary with sea conditions. Make sure your most qualified *helmsman* is steering the boat when conditions are bad.

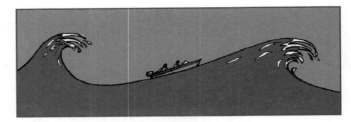

Figure 17. Boat Running Before Waves.

96 **Running before the waves** in a planing boat requires keeping the stern square to the waves and running on the back of a single wave. Use engine power to maintain a position about a third of the way back from the wave's crest. Be ready to adjust speed—faster or slower—to maintain steerage and control. In a slow displacement vessel, it can be difficult to stay with a single wave.

97 If you cannot stay with a single wave, concentrate on keeping the boat centered with its stern square to the waves coming up behind you, allowing successive waves to pass under your keel. Beware of larger waves crashing over the stern.

98 **Running parallel to the waves** is often uncomfortable and very dangerous. Even relatively small waves can start a pendulum motion in your boat if they strike you on the *beam* (from the side). A boat handles better heading into the waves rather than running parallel with them. If the spacing between successive waves happens to coincide with

Figure 18. Boat Broaching.

the natural roll period of the boat, each successive wave can give an additional push, resulting in greater and greater roll until the boat actually rolls over. This is called *broaching*. To avoid this, you may find it necessary to head into the waves in a direction somewhat away from your destination. By taking a course that is easier on the boat and on you, you may actually be able to travel faster and get there sooner (and less weary) than if you traveled the most direct route.

99 **Crossing the large wakes** of other vessels is inevitable. A wake is essentially a wave. Always alert your crew when you see a wake coming. Minimize the effect by reducing speed and turning into the waves at the proper angle for your boat. An unexpected wave can toss people around in the cockpit or cabin, or even overboard. Injuries or even death may result.

Figure 19. Large Wake Striking Boat Stern

100 **Stopping.** Boats have no brakes. You must take the engine out of gear and let it coast to a stop, or put the engine in reverse to stop short. Practice with your boat to determine the stopping distance at various speeds. Always come to a stop gradually. This will allow your stern wave to subside, and avoid your being *swamped* or tossed against the pier or another boat.

101 **Large vessels** and long barge tows require great distances to stop. Give way to these vessels and stay as far away as possible. Large vessels often create a dangerous rolling wake, and they can create disturbances in the water for thousands of feet behind them. Moored vessels may start their engines without warning. Other activities around a moored vessel

can create conditions dangerous to small craft in the vicinity.

102 Five or more short blasts on a ship's whistle is a danger signal. If you hear this, immediately look around to see if it is for you. If it is, get out of the way as quickly as possible consistent with safety. Use your VHF marine radio to talk with large ships if necessary to avoid a potentially dangerous situation.

103 **Weather Conditions.** Listen to weather forecasts while on the water. A day that starts out as clear and sunny can turn threatening in the afternoon as thunderstorms develop. Weather systems do not remain in one spot, but move across the earth's surface. Conditions can change with amazing speed.

102 Check the horizon frequently for signs of changing weather, and check the National Weather Service broadcasts frequently on the WX channels of your marine radio. (You may be able to hear weather messages on different channels. Make sure you are listening to the one that applies to the area where you are boating.) Keep an eye to the west, as weather usually changes from that direction. High, dark clouds or a change in wind direction or velocity may be indicators of threatening weather. Excessive static on an AM radio is usually a warning of thunderstorms in the area. If you suspect stormy weather, try to find a safe harbor.

103 **Preparing for Bad Weather.** Even a cautious skipper is caught in bad weather occasionally. If forced to ride out a storm, the following procedures are recommended:

• Put on life preservers. Most persons lost in boating accidents are not wearing life preservers. Use safety harnesses on a sailboat.

• Assign the best helmsman to steer the boat. Meet the waves at a speed and angle best for the boat under existing conditions. Practice determines the correct crossing angle for your hull—the angle varies with sea conditions. About

45° off the bow is common for small boats. Take special care when taking waves on the stern or broadside. On a sunny day, discover how your boat reacts under such circumstances.

- Find the best speed for boat control. Slow speed can decrease steering control. Finding the correct speed requires practice and will vary with the conditions.
- Batten down your vessel. Secure all hatches and ports. In a sailboat, reduce sail area. Fasten down all loose gear. In a small boat, seat your passengers in the bottom of the boat, as close to the centerline as possible.
- Check your bilge for water—keep it dry. Water is heavy and affects the stability of the boat.
- Know where you are and the location of the closest safe harbor. Choose the safest course—it may not be the shortest route. Always steer away from hazardous ground.

104 **Wind.** The hull and superstructure of a boat can act as a sail. Wind pressure on these areas will affect steering. Many powerboats have little hull below the waterline to resist the forces of wind. Wind from the side creates leeway, a sideways motion of the boat through the water. This is especially true when running slowly. Over a period of time this can have a serious effect on the accuracy of your intended course. Correct the problem by increasing speed slightly and steering more toward the wind. You will need practice to make the correction necessary to maintain your desired course.

105 **Hazards.** Check your chart to see if navigational aids identify known hazards. Follow your progress on the chart, and watch for buoys or daymarks. Dams present special hazards and may be difficult to see from upstream. There are usually warning signs, buoys or daymarks. However, there may be none. If so, stay well clear of the dam. Current becomes stronger close to the dam and the water is typically deeper. Anchoring in an emergency may be difficult. The area below a dam should also be avoided. The discharge of water creates turbulence and eddies that could cause you to lose control of your boat. Your boat could capsize.

106 Areas of whitewater create problems similar to those of a dam. It may be difficult to see whitewater areas from upstream until it's too late and you are drawn into the turbulence.

Docking

107 You can tell about boaters' abilities by observing how they leave and return to a pier or mooring.

108 **Plan in Advance.** As with getting under way, plan your approach to a dock or pier. You will have more control of your boat if you approach against the wind or current. Anticipate what might happen and have an idea of what you will do to recover.

109 Tell your crew what you want them to do before getting close to the dock. Install fenders on the appropriate side of the boat. Train someone to handle the dock lines, which should be coiled and ready. Hand dock lines to dock attendants if at all possible. If it is necessary to throw the lines, toss them underhanded close to one side of the attendants, never directly at them.

110 Alert your passengers to keep bodies, arms, and legs inside the boat. A *boat hook* is helpful for placing lines on pilings or cleats, but neither a boat hook nor a person will be able to stop the momentum of a heavy boat.

111 Make your approach cautiously and slowly, with just enough speed to maintain control. You do not want to plow into the pier, and you want to avoid having your own wake pound you against the pilings.

112 Sailboats should approach a dock under power when so equipped.

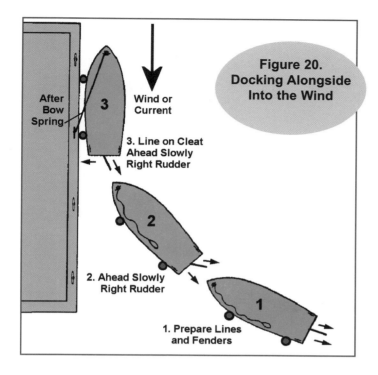

Figure 20. Docking Alongside Into the Wind

Wind or Current

After Bow Spring

3

3. Line on Cleat Ahead Slowly Right Rudder

2

2. Ahead Slowly Right Rudder

1

1. Prepare Lines and Fenders

113 **Docking Techniques.** With wind or current ahead or astern, docking is not usually a problem. Maneuver to approach into the wind or current. The bow line should be the first line to the pier or piling and long enough to become the *after-bow-spring line*

Figure 21. Docking Alongside Wind Off the Pier with Outboard or Stern Drive

Wind

Bow Line on Cleat

3

3. Reverse Engine Full Left Rudder Pull Stern In

2

2. Approach Pier, Bow Line Ready

1

1. Prepare Lines and Fenders

as seen in Figure 20. Loop it over a *piling*, or fasten it to a *cleat* on the pier, and move the boat slowly ahead. With the rudder or outdrive turned, the stern usually moves toward the pier. Use a similar method with an inboard-engined boat.

114 With wind or current on the pier, ease your boat up near the pier and let the wind blow you in to it.

115 With outboard or stern-drive boats and with wind or current off the pier, approach at an angle of about 15°–20° and fasten a *bow line* to the pier. Put the engine in reverse and turn the outdrive or outboard to bring the stern to the pier where a *stern line* can be fastened. The only way you will become proficient in docking is to practice with your boat.

Tying Up

116 It is important for the safety and security of your boat to know how to tie a boat properly to a pier, float, or mooring buoy.

117 **Lines.** You can seek advice from your marine dealer as to the proper size dock lines for your boat. The size of a cleat usually implies the diameter of line which the boat's manufacturer considers to be adequate. In general, never use lines smaller than 3/8 inch; handling a line of smaller diameter than this is difficult. With a boat 25 to 30 feet in length, 1/2-inch line is appropriate. 5/8-inch line is suitable for vessels of 35 to 40-feet in length. If in doubt, use a larger size, as long as it fits the cleats on the vessel.

118 Three strand nylon line is good for many uses because it provides some elasticity. Keep lines clean of mud, dirt, and grease. Coil lines to prevent kinking that can weaken the line. Store line in a dry place, out of direct sunlight.

119 **Knots and Hitches.** Boaters are traditionally supposed to be good at tying knots and hitches. The fact is, they really only need to

know two or three knots, but they need to be very good at tying those. In common usage, a *knot* is tied in a single line, a *hitch* secures a line to another object, and a *bend* joins two lines.

**Figure 22.
Round Turn
and
Two Half-Hitches**

120 A commonly used knot is the *round turn* with two *half-hitches*. The round turn (a simple wrap of a line around a post) takes the strain, and the two half hitches keep the round turn from falling off. It tends to slip, however, so many prefer the clove hitch and two half-hitches.

Figure 23. Clove Hitch

121 The *clove hitch* is similar to two round turns, but the over-and-under arrangement allows the line to bind itself against the object (piling, etc.), making it secure enough on its own to tie up your boat for short periods. Many boaters use the clove hitch to tie fenders to handrails. It can be finished off with a couple of half hitches to make it permanent.

122 A variation of the clove hitch is the *cleat hitch* as shown in Figure 24. Begin by taking a turn around the base of the cleat (the strong part of the cleat), then do one figure-eight around the horns of the cleat and finish off

Figure 24. Cleat Hitch

with a half-hitch. The result is a clove hitch around the two horns of the cleat: very secure, yet easy to undo. Under normal circumstances this holds a boat to the dock. Add another half-hitch if strong winds, currents or surges are expected.

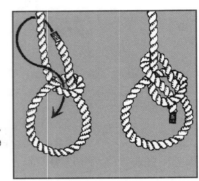

**Figure 25.
Bowline**

123 A slightly more complicated knot, but one with an infinite number of potential uses, is the *bowline* (pronounced BOW-lin as in bow and arrow). A bowline results in a fixed loop in the end of a line of whatever desired size that will not slip or tighten up. It is used to slide over a piling or around the horns of a cleat. It is the knot of choice for securing a lifeline about your waist. Many people use bowlines to tie to almost any object.

Figure 26. Figure-Eight Stopper Knot

124 For lines passing through pulleys, blocks or fairleads, add a stopper knot to keep loose ends from slipping through. An excellent stopper knot is the *figure-eight* knot.

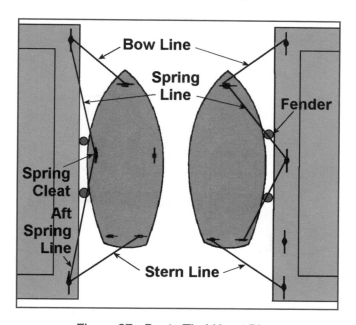

Figure 27. Boats Tied Up at Piers

125 **Tying to Piers and Floats.** To tie a boat alongside a pier properly requires a minimum of four dock lines — a bow line, a stern line, and two spring lines. Spring lines keep a boat from moving ahead or astern and, in tidal waters, allow the boat to move up and down relative to the pier. Keep the engine running until the boat is tied securely to the pier so that if something goes wrong the boat can still be controlled. Fasten the bow line, stern line, and spring lines as shown in Figure 27. The boat to the left has midship spring cleats. This allows two spring lines to be run from the pier to the boat. The boat to the right does not have spring cleats so the spring lines are run to the pier from the boat's bow and stern. In either case the boat is held away from the pier by suitable fenders. Lines must be long enough to allow some movement.

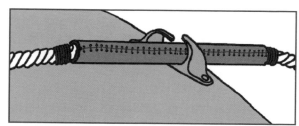

Figure 28. Chafing Gear on Line

126 Any boat tied up for long periods should use chafing gear where lines run through chocks. A chock is a fitting to guide a line. *Chafing gear* is sacrificial wrapping placed around lines, rigging, or spars to prevent wear. It is often made of cloth, cord, tape, leather, rubber, or plastic tubing.

127 When adjusting the length of dock lines in tidal areas, consider *tidal range* (the difference in height of water between any successive low and high *tide*).

128 **Leaving the Boat.** Never jump from a boat onto a pier. Make sure of your footing. Beware of slippery wet surfaces. Pass your gear onto the pier, then step ashore. Do not try to carry gear out of the boat and onto the pier. If the gear is too heavy to handle easily, rig a suitable gang plank.

129 **Tying to a Mooring Buoy.** Mooring *buoys* are permanent moorings and are the only buoys to which you may legally tie your boat. (It is illegal to tie any boat to a navigational aid.)

130 Permanent moorings usually have five parts:
1. anchor.
2. chain *rode.*
3. surface buoy attached to the *rode.*
4. mooring *pendant* attached to the buoy
5. small pickup float attached to the *pendant*

131 A pendant ("pen-ant") is a short line that serves as an extension of a mooring rode and actually attaches to the boat.

131 **Picking Up a Mooring.** Approach a mooring buoy slowly and with the boat under control, *heading* into the wind or current, whichever has the greater effect on the boat. Watch the position of the boat with respect to the mooring line. It is very easy to catch the mooring anchor rode or the pendant in the propeller or rudder.

Anchors and Anchoring

132 Every boater should master the art of anchoring. Without a well-set anchor, you will find yourself drifting into other boats or onto rocks or beaches. If you drift into other vessels and *foul* their anchors or damage their boats, you are responsible for damages.

133 **Choose the Correct Anchor.** The anchor you need will not only depend on the size and type of your boat, but upon the types of seabed and the amount of wind and current you expect to encounter.

134 No one type of anchor is best for all conditions. Each has strengths and weaknesses. As a starting point, watch what fellow boaters in your area use. While local knowledge is always valuable, only personal experience in anchoring your boat will tell you if you have made the correct choice.

135 Factors affecting the holding power of an anchor include design, weight, and material of construction. Anchors almost always hold by digging into the bottom, seldom by weight alone. Design strongly influences an anchor's ability to hook itself into the bottom.

136 **Lightweight anchors** are usually known by the names of their manufacturers and have long sharp flukes that pivot and bury completely under strain. They tend to work through soft bottoms down to firmer ground. They provide good holding power for their weight in sand, gravel, and mud. They may not hold well in grassy, rocky, or clay bottoms. Danforth®, Fortress®, West Marine®,

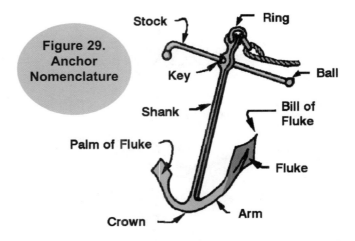

Figure 29. Anchor Nomenclature

Stock — Ring — Ball — Key — Bill of Fluke — Shank — Palm of Fluke — Fluke — Crown — Arm

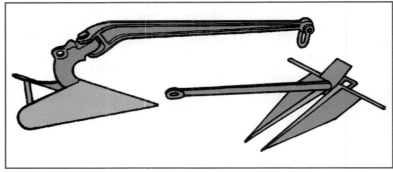

Figure 30. Plow Anchor (Left) Lightweight Anchor (Right)

Hooker®, and Suncor® are examples of this style anchor.

137 Plow anchors are popular with cruisers because they perform well in many different bottoms. They penetrate and hold well in weeds, grass, sand, mud, and gravel, although not as well in deep soft mud. Larger sizes are required for a given boat size. They are most easily stowed on a bow roller.

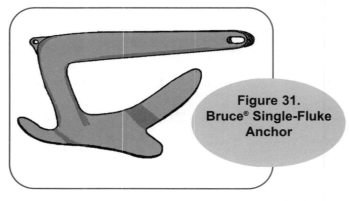

Figure 31. Bruce® Single-Fluke Anchor

138 **Single fluke anchors**, such as the Bruce® (Figure 31), hold well in most bottoms including rock and coral. They tend to reset without breaking out as the boat swings due to changes in wind or current direction. They are most easily stowed on a bow roller. Be aware, however, that in some jurisdictions it is illegal to damage coral with an anchor of any type.

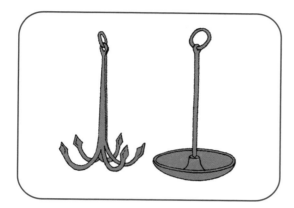

Figure 32. Grapnel (Left)
Mushroom Anchor (Right)

139 **Grapnels** have four or more thin arms, and are often used to retrieve lost objects, to snag projections on the seabed, or even to hang in trees to anchor a boat. A grapnel (Figure 32) has poor holding power in mud, sand, and gravel, but is good in rocks.

140 **Mushroom** anchors (Figure 32) are ideal for permanent mooring. They are often used to anchor permanent structures in soft sea beds. They sink deeply into the bottom if left for long periods, and when so embedded, have tremendous holding power.

141 Mushroom anchors are also used in small fishing boats, where they drag on the bottom and slow down the rate of drift for short periods of time, but they are not particularly good for anchoring overnight.

142 Attach a *trip line* to any anchor used where it is likely to snag on bottom features (stumps, debris, etc.). A trip line is a buoyed line attached to the crown of an anchor used to pull the anchor free when fouled.

143 Anchors are made in an assortment of sizes for various boats. Experienced boaters carry at least two anchors of different designs that will handle most different conditions. With two anchors, if you lose one, you have a back-up. Attach each anchor to its *rode* and carry them where they will be ready for instant use. (*Rode* is the nautical term for anchor line.)

144 Never anchor by the stern alone. In some situations an anchor over the stern can be used to keep a boat from swinging in a crowded harbor, but allowing a small boat to swing on a stern anchor is very dangerous. When windy, waves can overwhelm a small boat and enter the boat over the transom, especially if it has a cutout for an outboard motor.

145 **Rode.** A rode may be nylon rope or chain or a combination of the two. Nylon rope is strong, with good resistance to chafing and rubbing. It can stretch without damage to its fibers and will not rot when *stowed* wet. It is easy on the hands and does not float. These qualities make it ideal for a rode.

146 Chain is excellent as anchor rode on larger vessels. Although expensive and heavy, it has great strength and stows compactly. See Chapman *Piloting, Seamanship & Small Boat Handling* or other reference books for details on anchor rode materials.

147 The length of rode you should carry depends upon the depth of water in the areas where you will be anchoring. Carry a rode at least 10 times the depth of the water where you will be anchoring as explained later.

148 **Anchor Systems.** A length of chain installed between a rope rode and the anchor will improve holding power of an anchor. The chain lies on the bottom and keeps the direction of the pull of the rode more nearly horizontal. Chain also pro-

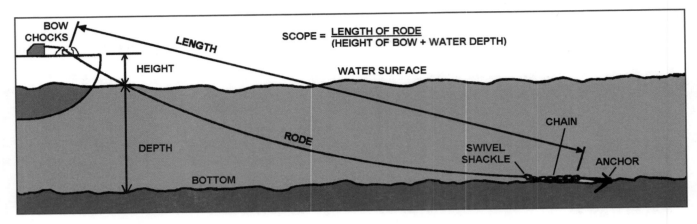

Figure 33. Anchor Scope

tects the rode from the effects of abrasion with objects on the bottom.

149 **Anchoring Techniques.** A rode must be relatively long compared to the vertical distance from the point of attachment on the boat to the bottom. This is necessary to achieve a nearly horizontal pull on the anchor. The ratio of the length of the rode to this vertical distance to the bottom is called *scope.*

150 Note that the vertical distance to the bottom includes:
1. the height of the bow of the boat from the surface of the water;
2. the depth of the water;
3. any anticipated difference in water depth due to rise and fall of the tide or changes in the level of a pool above a dam. The scope required depends on your anchor's ability to hold a particular type of bottom, considering wind and sea conditions.

151 Workable scope will vary from a minimum of about 5:1 for calm conditions to 10:1 or more in severe conditions. 7:1 is generally suitable for most situations. For example:
- You wish to anchor in 10 feet of water using a scope of 7:1.
- The bow of your boat is 3 feet above the surface of the water.

- You expect the tide to rise 5 feet while you are anchored.
- You need at least 126 feet of rode. ([10 + 5 + 3] x 7 = 126).

If severe weather develops, increase your scope to at least 10:1, using 180 feet of rode or more. The longer the line, the shallower the angle of pull, and the easier the anchor will dig in. In a storm, the elasticity of the longer line will also help cushion the boat against wave action. In restricted anchoring conditions make certain you leave room for the boat to swing.

152 **Setting an Anchor.** Approach the place you intend to anchor against the wind or current, whichever has more effect on your boat. When you reach the desired position, bring the boat to a standstill. Lower (never throw) the anchor to the bottom over the bow. Allow the boat to drift with the wind or current, or apply slow reverse power if necessary, and pay out line.

153 Let the rode out slowly to keep it from fouling the anchor. Make sure the line does not wrap around your legs as you pay it out. Use more rode than you need for your planned scope to increase the horizontal pull necessary to dig in the anchor. When sufficient line is out, snub it by taking a turn around your bow cleat, then place an easy strain on the line with the engine.

154 As a general rule, if the anchor does not hold, pay out more line until the anchor bites. In order to help in this regard, consider marking the line in advance at ten-foot intervals so you can judge how much anchor rode has been *paid out*.

155 When you are satisfied that the anchor is set (dug in), take in any extra rode, run it through a *chock*, and tie it to the bow cleat with a cleat hitch. Always observe the relationship of the boat to objects on shore, and check periodically to see that the anchor is not dragging.

156 **Retrieving an Anchor.** When ready to hoist anchor, approach the anchor position slowly, taking in the line to avoid fouling it around your boat's propeller or rudder. When your pull on the anchor line is straight up-and-down, it should break out easily. If it is deeply embedded, it may be necessary to *snub* the rode around the bow cleat and run the boat gently forward, breaking it out with engine power. If that is not successful, move the boat slowly in a circle, taking extreme care that the anchor line is kept away from propellers and rudders.

Water Sport Safety

157 For whatever reason you use a watercraft, all water sports require certain knowledge and skills to be enjoyed safely.

158 Participants in water sports should be good swimmers, but they should wear life jackets whenever on the water. Federal regulations require that every vessel carry at least one Coast Guard-approved life jacket for every person on board. In addition, boats 16 feet long or longer are required to carry at least one Coast Guard-approved throwable flotation device (ring buoy, horseshoe, cushion).

159 It is strongly recommended that each individual be assigned a personal life jacket; that they try it on and adjust it to fit. If you have children on board, make sure you have life-jackets in the proper size. Adult jackets may be too large. Small children, especially, may need special life jackets with crotch straps to keep the jacket from riding up over their heads and coming off in the water.

Special Gear

160 Some water sports such as ski jumping and personal watercraft (PWC) riding can involve high-speed falls. Wear a helmet and a life jacket designed to withstand high-speed impact with the water without coming off or disintegrating.

Personal Care

161 Your enjoyment of boating, as well as your safety, depend in large measure on how well you are protected from the effects of exposure to the environment. Even people who are in excellent physical condition and accustomed to spending long hours on the water in the fresh air and sunshine find that their reactions and judgment are impaired after a few hours. Those of us who lead more sedentary lives during the week may need to take special precautions.

162 Protect yourself from the elements with appropriate clothing; eat well; drink plenty of water; and avoid alcohol while engaging in water sports. Consider taking a first aid course.

163 If age or health is an issue for you or for your family or crew, or if you frequently encounter stressful weather conditions, you may want to consider these factor in your choice of a boat. If you have small children, for example, you may want to select a boat that provides some shelter from sun and rain, such as a cuddy cabin, rather than an open runabout.

Know the Waters in Your Area

164 Falls in shallow water can result in injuries due to rocks, trash, or just the bottom. Adverse currents can take you way off

course. Stay in safe waters, especially as you learn your water sport.

Hours of Operation

165 Many areas, especially on small lakes, regulate hours of operation. These may apply to all boats, or only to certain types such as powerboats or PWCs. The purpose of these rules is to improve boating safety and/or reduce noise during certain hours.

Night Activity

166 If you operate a boat at night (i.e., any time between sunset and sunrise) show the required lights to let other boaters know you are there. Traveling at high speed in the limited visibility of darkness can be dangerous, and in some areas illegal. Never engage in water sports (except fishing) at night.

Know What to Do in an Emergency

167 Do not abandon your equipment in an emergency. Water skis, an ice chest or even an overturned boat will float you, and will provide a target more easily seen in the water than your head alone. Carry a whistle or a horn to use if in need of help. Signal for help by slowly and repeatedly raising arms outstretched to each side.sport.

Fishing and Hunting

168 People who hunt and fish on the water have one of the highest boating fatality rates. Many consider their boat as simply part of their hunting and fishing gear. The standard safety rules that apply to all boating also apply to hunters and fishers.

- Check the weather before you go and make sure someone knows where you are going and when you plan to return.
- Always wear a life preserver (PFD—Personal Flotation Device).
- Don't stand in the boat.
- Don't overload the boat.
- Stow firearms and hunting knives properly.

- Assign shooting and casting areas for each person in the boat to avoid accidents with others in the boat.
- Wearing waders can be dangerous. If you fall overboard, waders can fill with water making it impossible to get back in or up an embankment. If you wear waders while launching a boat, remove them prior to leaving the launch area.
- Never use alcohol while boating.

Personal Watercraft

169 **A personal watercraft is a boat.** The United States Coast Guard considers personal watercraft (PWC) to be Class A (less than 16 feet in length) inboard boats. Anyone who operates a PWC is a skipper with the same responsibilities as the operator of a 40 foot yacht. Operators must adhere to many of the same rules and regulations as larger boats.

170 Persons riding personal watercraft should always be good swimmers.

171 **The Personal Watercraft Industry Association** defines a PWC as an inboard vessel less than 13 feet in length that uses an internal combustion engine powering a water-jet pump as its primary source of propulsion. It has no open load-carrying area that could retain water, and is designed to be operated with a person or persons positioned on, rather than within, the confines of the hull. Because of their different operating characteristics, some states consider PWCs to be a special type of boat and have special regulations for them.

172 **PWC Load Capacity:** As with other small craft, PWC manufacturers provide information as to the maximum carrying capacity of the vessel. The number of seating positions determines the maximum allowable number of people a PWC should carry. However, the total combined weight of people and equipment may limit the number of riders to less than the number of seats. No vessel should

be overloaded, including a PWC. Overloading makes vessels difficult to steer and control and be unstable.

How a PWC Works

173 A water-jet pump draws water in through an underwater grate and forces it out the rear of the craft under high pressure. This pushes the boat through the water. At idle speed the craft will move very slowly. As the engine speed increases, it will go faster.

174 **Operator Controls.** Read and understand your PWC owner's manual before you ride. Have a qualified person give you instruction in its operation. Understand the function of all controls, where they are located, and how to use them.

175 **Steering.** Handlebars turn a movable nozzle that directs the high-pressure stream of water, either right or left, out of the nozzle at the stern which turns the boat to one side or the other.

176 It is important to know that a PWC will turn only when the jet pump is operating and pushing a stream of water out of the stern of the craft and creating thrust. If you release the throttle to avoid collision while operating at high speed, your PWC will not turn. It will probably continue in the direction you were moving, often into the object you were trying to avoid.

177 **Start and Stop Controls.** PWCs do not have ignition keys as do an automobiles. You push a button or switch on the handlebar or console to start and stop the engine. A manual choke control helps start a cold engine.

178 **Throttle Controls** are usually on the right handlebar grip. They can either be a "thumb-push" type or a "finger-pull" type.

179 **Fall-off Controls** are an aid to re-boarding your craft when you fall off. Some PWCs have an auto-circle control which slows the engine to idle speed and allows the craft to circle slowly. This permits you to swim to your PWC and reboard. If you have this type of control, be sure to set your idle speed correctly. Other PWCs have a lanyard cut-off switch (sometimes called a *life-line*) which will stop the engine if you fall off.

180 **Use of the Lanyard.** The lanyard is a cord with a short strap that is attached to the operator's wrist or life jacket (PFD) at one end. The other end of the strap is attached to a plug inserted into the switch that controls the ignition. If the operator falls off the PWC, the strap pulls the plug and stops the engine. The operator can then swim to the PWC and reboard.

181 Expect to fall off your PWC. It will not be dangerous if you follow the manufacturer's safety guidelines. If you fall, push away from the PWC.

182 **Fuel Selector Switches** usually have three positions; an *off* position for use when not riding, an *on* position to use when riding, and a *reserve* position to use to head straight for a fuel supply when fuel runs out in the *on* position. Fuel and oil gauges are standard equipment on some larger PWCs.

183 **Reverse Levers** on some PWCs close a *clamshell* device over the steering nozzle to allow slow reverse operation. Never use reverse as a brake or at high speeds (you could be thrown off and injured.)

184 **Righting an Overturned PWC.** If your craft rolls and floats upside down, roll it back upright as directed by the manufacturer. Look for a decal at the rear of the craft for instructions. If there is no decal, check your owner's manual. Turning it the wrong way could get water into the engine.

185 **Re-boarding.** It is important to practice getting back on board your PWC. Follow the manufacturer's instructions in your operating manual. Always practice reboarding in deep water.

186 **Stopping.** Since a PWC has no brakes, you must allow adequate distance in order to make a safe stop. The best way to stop is to spin your PWC (turn it in a tight circle).

Required PWC Equipment

187 Almost all governmental boating laws, regulations, and safety standards that apply to Class A boats apply to your PWC. We will discuss these more in Chapter 2. Required equipment consists of the following items.

- A wearable life preserver for each person onboard. Most practical is a Type III inherently buoyant flotation aid—although this type of preserver will not turn an unconscious victim face up in the water. Preservers should have an impact rating of at least 50 miles per hour (preferably in excess of the maximum speed of your craft).
- A fire extinguisher. Even though your PWC may be equipped with a container or bracket to hold a fire extinguisher, mount your fire extinguisher in the bracket that comes with the extinguisher and place it in the PWC container.
- A sound producing device. A small mouth-operated whistle attached to the operator's life jacket is ideal.

188 Although Visual Distress Signals (VDS) are not required for Class A boats, if you go offshore any farther than someone can see you waving for help (about one-half mile) carry a day-type VDS. (An orange distress flag is ideal.) Since in most cases it is illegal to operate your PWC after dark, night distress signals are unnecessary. The international distress signal of slowly and repeatedly raising outstretched arms to each side is a simple attention-getter.

PWC Regulations

189 You must register and number a PWC. The hull design of a PWC requires that registration numbers be placed high on the bow in a prominent position. The rules for size of letters and numbers and contrasting color are discussed in Chapter 2. Laminate your certificate so that it will not get wet.

190 Even though personal watercraft are exempt from the USCG standard requiring capacity plates on small boats, manufacturers often make recommendations as to the number of persons and the weight their craft can safely accommodate. Look for this information on a label on the craft and in the owner's manual. Never exceed these recommendations. An overloaded PWC will be unstable in the water and difficult to operate safely. You could be cited for reckless operation if you overload your craft and operate it dangerously.

Additional Safety Equipment

191 Local regulations often call for additional required equipment. Always check your local regulations for their requirements. In many states, you must wear a life preserver whenever aboard a PWC. Some states require day-type visual distress signals.

Optional Personal Equipment

192 For bodily protection you may want to consider special equipment such as:
- Sun-block for protection from the sun.
- Strap-on floating sun glasses or goggles for eye protection.
- Gloves to better grip the steering controls.
- Footwear to protect your feet while in the water.
- Helmets to protect your head from injury when falling.
- Wet suits to reduce the possibility of hypothermia and to protect the body from abrasion and injury. They are not, however, a substitute for a life preserver unless they have a CG approval label.

Operate Your PWC Safely

193 PWC operators must always be alert and vigilant when riding their craft. There are many things to think about when operating a craft that is so fast in speed and quick in response.

194 **Safe Speed.** A PWC is fast and sensitive and, under certain conditions, unstable. Don't dart about. Always operate at a speed at which you will have time to react and avoid a collision. Many states have laws limiting the speed of a boat when near shore. Maintain only minimum speed necessary to maintain steerageway when near shore, launch areas, swimming areas, docks, and anchored boats. No wake and slow speed zones are usually designated with markers. Observe them carefully. The speed limit in these restricted areas is often five mph or less.

195 **Jumping Wakes.** Part of the fun of operating a PWC is jumping waves. However, cutting close to the sterns of other boats and jumping their wakes is dangerous and often illegal. It is also a distraction to persons operating other boats.

196 When jumping a boat's wake, stay at least 100 feet behind the boat. This should allow you sufficient room to observe traffic conditions in all directions. Avoid jumping wakes in areas of heavy boat traffic. If you fall, you may not be seen in the water, and you could be injured by an approaching boat. Avoid cutting in front of other boats for the same reasons. Never follow closely behind another PWC when jumping wakes. If he falls, you may hit him. Remember, a PWC out of the water has no steering because of loss of pump suction.

197 Trick maneuvers are dangerous. They require skill and common sense and can result in failure to pay attention to surroundings. Accidents and injuries are often the result.

198 **Keep a Lookout.** Operators of PWCs are often so intent on operating the craft and having fun they fail to maintain a lookout. At high speed, they focus attention on the waves ahead, disregarding what is to each side and to the rear. This tunnel vision prevents them from seeing approaching boats, swimmers in the water, and hazards to navigation.

199 **Fatigue** is a major consideration when riding a PWC. Never overestimate your ability. Be certain your skills and physical condition are sufficient to handle any wind, wave, or distance-to-shore conditions you may encounter. If you fatigue easily, you may not want to ride alone. Be cautious when riding in areas of strong current and when it is windy. You may have difficulty getting back to your craft under these conditions.

200 It is good practice to schedule a 10-minute break on the beach for every 30 minutes of riding. If you become fatigued or start to feel cold, head for home. Your body is telling you that you are either running out of energy or that there is an abnormal lowering of your body's internal temperature due to exposure to cold air, wind, or water. This can lead to hypothermia.

201 **Observe Aids to Navigation.** The marks of the U.S. Aids to Navigation System and the Uniform State Waterway Marking System are the street signs and caution signs that guide all boaters in safe boating. We will discuss these in Chapter 3.

202 **Navigation Rules.** The speed and quick movement of a personal watercraft require an operator's constant attention to the surroundings to avoid collision. This is even more important when operating with other personal watercraft. Operators must know the Navigation Rules in order to make split-second decisions to avoid collision. We will study these rules in Chapter 3.

203 **Water Skiers.** Before towing water skiers with your PWC, check with state and local authorities to see if it is legal to do so. If you tow skiers, you must have a personal watercraft with capacity to carry three persons:
1. the operator.
2. the observer.
3. the skier and the skis when going to and returning from the ski area.

204 Always keep a distance from water skiers; never follow them or cross between them and the tow boat. Both you and the skier could have serious accidents.

205 **Fire Onboard.** If a fire occurs, stop your PWC immediately. Most fires occur in the engine compartment. Never open a closed engine compartment that contains a fire. It will introduce oxygen into the air which will fuel the fire. The best reaction to a fire in your PWC is to leave your craft and swim as far away from it as possible. Save your fire extinguisher to help other boaters.

206 **Breakdowns and Repairs.** As in other craft, there is always the possibility of mechanical breakdown, fires, and other emergencies. Thus, it is advisable to travel with other PWC operators.

207 Always keep your PWC in first-class operating condition. Keep the engine properly tuned, the battery fully charged, and all electrical connections clean and tight. You will be able to make very few repairs on the water. Opening your engine compartment in high wave conditions can swamp and sink your boat. If you cannot repair your PWC on the water, you will need a tow to shore. Carry a tow line in your equipment locker.

208 Debris such as plastic bags and seaweed can be sucked against the water intake grate. You will notice a severe reduction in thrust and speed. Never attempt to clear obstructions such as this with the engine running. Try rocking the craft back and forth. If this does not work, you may have to roll the craft over and remove the debris with your hands.

209 Keep hands, feet, hair, and clothing away from the water intake whenever the engine is running. If you don't, the results could be deadly.

210 **Security.** Try not to leave your PWC unattended. If you must leave it for any time, remove the stop-lanyard and carry it with you. Try to lock your craft to some immovable object with a chain and padlock. If you leave it on a trailer, add a trailer hitch lock. Removing one of the trailer wheels is another possible theft deterrent.

Considerate and Responsible Operation

211 Being aware, using good judgment, and having consideration for others are most important in operating a boat of any kind. Always think of the effect you have on others as you operate your PWC.

212 **Operate Quietly.** Making excessive noise is one of the quickest ways to make PWCs unpopular with other water users, as well as people on shore. It creates pressure to regulate PWC activity.

Try not to operate continuously in one area. Avoid residential areas, camping areas, and waterfronts; areas where people often go to be quiet. Local ordinances frequently limit the noise level of boat engines. Your PWC must be equipped with an effective muffling device. Altered mufflers are never permitted.

213 **Consider the Environment.** Be a responsible citizen and work towards the preservation of our fragile environment.

• Never throw trash or spill fuel or oil into the water.

• Try to operate in deep water as much as possible. When operating at high speeds, your PWC can disturb the delicate bottom in water six feet deep.

• Keep wake at a minimum when close to shore; it can contribute to shoreline erosion.

• Operating near the shoreline can disturb wildlife. Excessive noise disturbs birds as well as shoreline residents and other boaters.

Boating Courtesy

214 Let courtesy and common sense guide your actions on your boat just as it does anywhere else. The Golden Rule of "doing unto others as you would have them do unto you" is an excellent guide. Remember that noise carries a great distance on the water, particularly at night. If you anchor out, keep voices down, music low, and leave with a minimum of noise. High speed boating in restricted or congested areas is both dangerous and against the law.

215 Respect private property. If you experience a genuine emergency, owners of private piers and docks will almost certainly accommodate you until the emergency is past, but do not use private facilities without permission.

216 Give consideration to sailing vessels. Sailors have much less maneuverability than powerboaters, especially when there is little wind. Give sail races or powerboat navigation contests a wide berth. Go around them, not through them. Give wide berth to fishermen, and watch your wake. Conversely, neither sailboaters nor fishermen should obstruct narrow *channels*.

217 Rendering assistance to others in distress is not only common courtesy, but required by law, providing it does not endanger your own boat or crew. You are generally protected from liability if you act reasonably and prudently as a Good Samaritan.

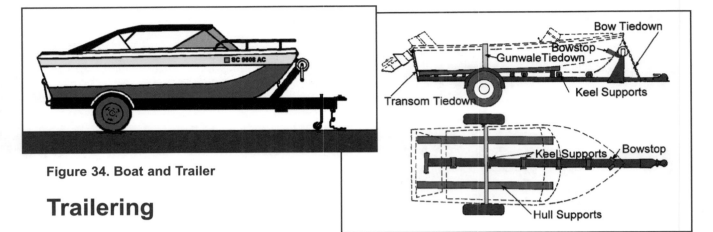

Figure 34. Boat and Trailer

Figure 35. Trailer Arrangement

Trailering

218 Trailering may seem a better topic for a highway safety course than for boaters. However, millions of boats are trailerable and for thousands of boaters every weekend, getting there is part of the boating experience.

The Trailer

219 There are two essential aspects to trailering:
1. The trailer.
2. The towing vehicle.

220 **The trailer must fit the boat.** Make sure that the boat and trailer fit one another. The trailer must have sufficient weight-carrying ability to support the boat, motor, fuel, and all the gear you plan to add to it, and it must also support the hull so the load is evenly distributed and the hull is not bent out of shape or stressed. There should be supports under the engine, fuel tanks, batteries, etc. Ideally, the boat and trailer are designed and engineered to work together.

221 **Trailer Winch.** Most boat trailers have a *winch* at the front with a cable or strap and a hook that can be attached to a strong fitting (the *bow eye*) on the *stem* of the boat to help load it. The strap or cable is under enormous strain during loading, so make certain that:

a. It is in excellent condition, with no kinks or frays.

b. Nobody is in direct line with the cable or strap, should it break and snap back.

If the winch is hand cranked, make certain the ratchet is engaged. A runaway winch handle can break bones.

222 **Tiedowns.** Provide some means of fastening the boat on to the trailer other than the winch cable. Use a separate chain, *turnbuckle*, or other fastening at the bow to keep the boat from sliding backward off the trailer. Add other tiedowns to keep the boat from sliding forward into the back of the towing vehicle in a sudden stop. In addition, use straps or other sturdy tiedowns to keep the stern of the boat on the trailer at rough crossings or potholes.

223 Make certain all tiedowns are tight and secure when the boat and trailer are being moved, but loosen them if the boat is going to be sitting on the trailer for an extended period (such as over-winter storage) to avoid distorting the hull.

The Tow Vehicle

224 Check with your manufacturer or dealer for information concerning the type of vehicle and the options you will need to tow your boat. In general, front-wheel drive vehicles are suitable only for the smallest, lightest boats. (Remember to include the weight of the trailer, fuel, and any other added equipment into the calculations when you estimate your towing requirements.)

225 Options you may need to consider include:

- heavy-duty suspension.
- extra engine cooling capacity.
- separate transmission and oil coolers.
- additional electrical generating capacity.
- outside mirrors.
- trailer light wiring harness and trailer brake connections.
- heavy-duty turn signal flasher (prevents rapid blinking).

226 **Trailer Hitches.** Make sure the hitch you plan to use is adequate and appropriate. Hitches are either load carrying or load distributing; some trailers are designed to be used with one type of hitch, and using the other type may damage the trailer. Basic hitches are shown in Figure 34 along with gross towing loads.

227 Use the correct size hitch ball and safety chains. These chains keep the trailer connected to the tow vehicle in case the hitch or ball breaks, and should be crossed from one side to the other underneath the hitch to cradle the trailer tongue and keep it off the road surface if the ball hitch breaks or

Closed Threaded Link

Figure 37. Crossed Chains at Hitch

loosens. Some states require that "S" hooks be replaced by a more secure form of connection that will not accidentally come loose from the towing vehicle. Review your state's trailering laws as well as those of states you plan to drive through.

228 The amount of trailer tongue weight on a hitch ball is critical. It should be about 10% of the weight of the rig when the coupler is parallel to the ground. Too much weight will lower the rear of the tow vehicle. That will increase tire wear, make the vehicle difficult to steer and reduce the effectiveness of the

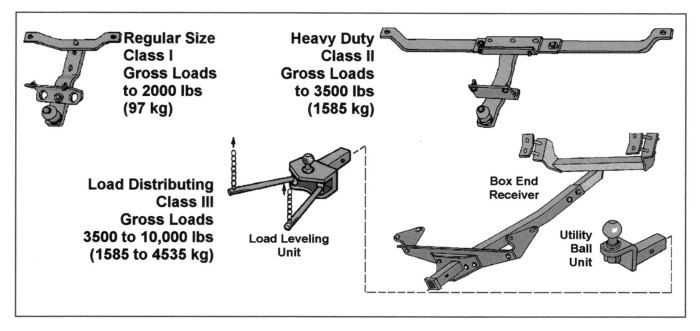

Regular Size Class I Gross Loads to 2000 lbs (97 kg)

Heavy Duty Class II Gross Loads to 3500 lbs (1585 kg)

Load Distributing Class III Gross Loads 3500 to 10,000 lbs (1585 to 4535 kg)

Load Leveling Unit

Box End Receiver

Utility Ball Unit

Figure 36. Trailer Hitch Classes

brakes. Too little weight will cause the trailer to fishtail and is dangerous.

Driving With a Trailer

229 Driving with a trailer is not the same as driving the vehicle alone. The combination is heavier and longer. It occupies more room on the highway and needs much longer to stop. Even if the trailer has brakes of its own, you must learn to think even farther ahead than usual. You must anticipate changes in traffic flow far enough in advance to respond.

230 Assemble a kit of tools to deal with highway emergencies. Things to consider carrying include:

• hazard flares and/or reflectors.

• wheel chocks

• a jack capable of lifting the trailer *and* the boat. (A typical car jack *will not* work on a trailer. Make sure the jack will fit under the trailer axle or frame with a flat tire.)

• spare tire and wheel, wheel bearings, light bulbs, etc.

• a tire gauge covering the range of pressures needed for your trailer tires (trailer tires often carry pressures well in excess of those found in automobile tires).

231 Underinflated trailer tires will not track well behind the towing vehicle—and worse—they will overheat, leading to blowouts.

232 Take frequent rest breaks (once an hour, at least). Driving with a trailer is more stressful than driving the vehicle alone, and you need frequent breaks to stay fresh and alert. Use your rest breaks to walk around and inspect your vehicle, trailer, and boat. Check everything including your tiedowns, hitch connections, etc. Feel tires and hubs. If the tires or hubs feel warmer than usual, you may have a problem, such as tire underinflation or bearing failure. It is usual for tandem-axle trailers with brakes to have brakes on only one axle. If that is the case, the wheel with the brakes will normally be warmer than the wheel with-

out the brakes. Experience is a great teacher when it comes to towing a boat on a trailer.

233 **Reduce Your Speed.** Speed limits for vehicles with trailers are usually lower than they are for cars alone, and many trailer manufacturers' warranties are void if you exceed their speed limit.

234 **Backing a trailer** is not difficult, if you approach it correctly. Find an open paved space (a shopping center parking lot during off hours is ideal). Set up cardboard boxes (preferably empty) as markers, and practice. Do not let many people offer you advice; find out for yourself what works for you. In any case, move slowly, and if you fail, analyze what happened, what went wrong, then try again. The towing vehicle pivots around the rear axle as the front wheels are steered. This causes the trailer move in the opposite direction and requires a gentle touch to cause the trailer to go where you want it to go. Backing the vehicle to the left causes the trailer to go to the right and vice versa.

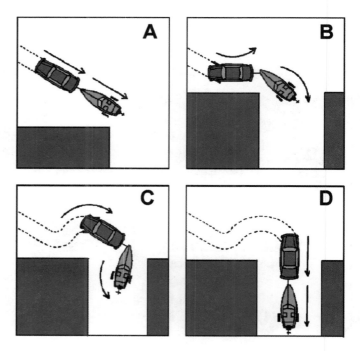

Figure 38. Backing a Trailer

235 Do as much maneuvering as possible while moving forward. In other words, align yourself as much as possible while you are pulling forward so you are backing straight to your destination.

236 **Launching Your Boat.** Launching ramps are busy places, and there is a lot of competition for ramp space. Areas are usually reserved for launch preparations such as removing covers, tiedowns, etc., from the boat. Install bilge plugs, hang fenders, place dock lines, prepare any other equipment you need to launch. Finally, you will be using the vehicles brakes during the launch so disconnect your trailer light connection so the hot bulbs will not shatter when they become immersed in the cold water.

237 Check overhead for wires and other obstructions, especially if your boat is a sailboat with the mast raised.

238 Back slowly down the ramp until the boat begins to float off its supports, but if possible avoid getting any part of the towing vehicle in the water. Use wheel chocks on steep ramps. You are parked on a hill (the ramp) and many vehicles are accidentally launched every year.

239 Warning. Never leave children or any other passengers or pets in the towing vehicle during the launch. They may not be able to escape, should the vehicle accidentally roll into the water.

240 After the boat is floating and secured (either tied to a pier or held by someone capable), pull the trailer straight out of the ramp and move it to the parking area. Clear the ramp area as quickly as possible for other users, but do not rush so much that you forget important steps or take risks. It is often a considerable distance from the launch ramp to the location for tow vehicle parking.

241 **Recovering Your Boat.** When you recover your boat, make certain that the boat is aligned with the trailer and will eventually rest straight and even on its supports. You may not be able to pull the boat all the way up on the trailer with the winch alone without creating excess strain on the boat or the trailer. If that is the case, you may choose to pull it on by stages, winching the boat up a bit, then backing farther into the water, winching it further on, and so on, until the boat is fully on the trailer and straight on the supports. This often requires a team effort with one person at the winch and the other carefully operating the tow vehicle.

242 Check again for overhead obstructions, and lower antennas, masts, etc., as necessary to clear. Make sure the motor or outdrive lower unit is raised enough that it will not hit the ramp, then pull the boat and trailer straight out of the ramp to an area where you can complete rigging the trailer for the highway.

243 Once in the rigging area, remove and store the bilge drain plug, take in and stow all lines and fenders, and wipe down the hull if necessary. If you were in salt water, flush the motor's cooling system and wash the lower unit, trailer and vehicle with fresh water as soon as possible. Some motors and some trailers are equipped with special flushing connections to rinse out internal passages. See if fresh water hose connections are provided at the launch site.

244 Finally, off-load anything that needs to ride in the vehicle (don't overload the boat and trailer), reconnect the trailer tail and stoplights and test them (don't forget turn signals), Perform one more walk-around inspection looking for missed items, and head for home.

Theft Prevention

245 Theft *of* boats and *from* boats is a major problem. Boats are often left unattended for days at a time, and it is not uncommon for thieves to slip into a harbor by dark of night in the middle of the week, cut lines and tow a boat out without anybody being the wiser for several days, by which time the boat can be long gone. No nationwide system exists for tracing and identifying boats, such as there is for motor vehicles. You cannot stop a determined and professional thief, but you can slow him down and perhaps discourage him enough that he will look for easier prey.

246 Boats usually cannot be locked up as securely as a house, and they often have valuable equipment on board that is easy to sell and hard to trace. Keep valuable items, particularly portable items, out of sight. If your boat is open and accessible by design, arrange to take valuables with you whenever you leave your boat.

247 Prepare a detailed list (with serial numbers) of equipment and personal items that you have on board, and file it with your insurance papers in a safe place on shore. Then check with your insurance agent to be sure of your coverage, and follow all recommendations. There are locks available to help secure outboard motors, trailer hitches, etc. Use them. Add a padded chain and a secure lock to the mooring lines securing your boat to the pier or trailer. Consider adding a hidden ignition cutout switch or a lockable fuel cutoff valve.

248 If you install a security alarm, choose one that is designed for use on a boat. Automobile alarms often are designed to be triggered by the current flowing to overhead dome lights when a door is opened, etc., and can be set off by automatic bilge pumps. Some also respond to movement, as when a car is hoisted on a wrecker, and can be triggered by the normal rocking of the boat. The components in an automobile alarm are not intended for a marine environment and may include materials that will deteriorate quickly in salt air.

249 Perhaps the best protection against theft is other boaters. Know your neighbors and make sure they know you. Keep an eye out for strangers, and ask your neighbors (especially those who may live aboard or visit their boats during the week) to do the same for you.

Getting Started • Review

Name .... Date .... Group No. ....

1. The lowest part of the hull interior is the:
   a. helm.
   b. cuddy.
   c. quarter.
   d. bilge.

2. The widest part of the hull is called:
   a. the quarter.
   b. the LOA.
   c. the beam.
   d. the tiller.

3. The measurement of how deeply a boat's hull penetrates the water is its:
   a. draft.
   b. head.
   c. helm.
   d. beam.

4. Freeboard is the:
   a. right side of a boat when facing the bow.
   b. height of a boat's gunwale measured inside the cockpit.
   c. distance from the water to the lowest point of a boat where water could come aboard.
   d. provision of food and quarters for volunteer crews on ocean races.

5. A displacement hull is one that:
   a. moves through the water by pushing it aside.
   b. skims along the surface of the water.
   c. is capable of very high speeds.
   d. may easily capsize in heavy seas.

6. Three factors affect the seaworthiness and safety of a vessel: its design, construction materials, and:
   a. baggywrinkle.
   b. type of head.
   c. size.
   d. cockpit.

7. When shopping for a boat, the following important questions should be addressed:
   1. What type and style will best serve your use of a boat?
   2. How large a boat will you need for the number of persons accompanying you?, and 3. . . .
   a. Is a solid-state ignition preferable to one with a distributor, rotor, and points?
   b. Will you be boating in open seas or protected waters?
   c. What type of interior decor will please your family?
   d. Would a gasoline fueled engine be better than one that operates on diesel or propane fuel?

8. You should have on board charts of the area where you are boating to help you determine where you are and:
   a. provide you with up-to-date weather forecasts.
   b. show you where the fish are, if you are a fisherman.
   c. give you the location of near-by refreshment stands.
   d. where you want to be to avoid busy shipping lanes and hazards.

9. **A safety-conscious skipper never starts the engine on a boat before:**
   a. all passengers are comfortably seated on the foredeck, gunwale, or transom.
   b. checking to see that there is enough alcohol and additives in the fuel.
   c. checking the Sunday newspaper for a weather forecast.
   d. sniffing for fuel vapors in the engine and fuel compartments.

10. **Before fueling a boat with a built-in fuel tank, you should:**
    a. close all portholes, doors, and hatches.
    b. turn on the bilge blower, if so equipped.
    c. open all portholes, doors, and hatches.
    d. keep all smokers at least three feet away.

11. **In addition to keeping the pump nozzle in constant metal-to-metal contact with the filler pipe, an important safety instruction to follow when refilling portable fuel cans and tanks is to:**
    a. always use approved yellow marine safety tanks.
    b. take them out of the boat and fill them on the dock.
    c. use only approved safety tanks and fill them inside the boat.
    d. step carefully onto the gunwale when carrying full tanks aboard.

12. **A float plan includes a description of your boat, who is on board, your safety equipment, and, most importantly:**
    a. the name of your radio operator.
    b. where you expect to be and when you expect to return.
    c. the draft of your boat.
    d. what mechanical equipment on your boat is not in the best condition.

13. **Small boats are unstable, and falls are always a risk. Always step into the center of small boats; never on the:**
    a. boom.
    b. fender.
    c. gunwale.
    d. beam.

14. **Constantly watch the wake of your boat, because:**
    a. it can disturb the smooth operation of personal watercraft.
    b. your wake must never be more than three inches high.
    c. you are responsible for injuries or damage to property caused by the wake of your boat.
    d. you may see beautiful colors created by the oxidation of phosphorus in the water.

15. **When running into waves, ease the shock on boat and crew by slowing down and:**
    a. taking the waves at an angle to the bow, not head-on.
    b. turning the boat broadside to the waves for stability.
    c. taking the waves head-on and not at an angle.
    d. instruct all passengers to stand up in the boat.

16. **If you are caught on the water in bad weather, your first step should be to:**
    a. listen for a weather forecast.
    b. pour water into the bilge to increase stability.
    c. turn and head for shore at full speed.
    d. see that all aboard are wearing USCG-approved life preservers.

17. **When docking and undocking your boat it is desirable to plan the procedure in advance and:**
    a. always operate your boat at cruising speed.
    b. approach slowly against the wind or current for more control of your boat.
    c. shout instructions so the crew knows who is in charge.
    d. teach the crew how to keep the boat away from the pier using their arms and legs.

18. **A knot with an many potential uses that may be used to form a secure loop in the end of a line is the:**
    a. clove hitch.
    b. figure eight knot.
    c. cleat hitch.
    d. bowline.

19. **A spring line is a dock line that:**
    a. has an inner core of stretchy elastic material.
    b. keeps a boat from moving ahead or astern.
    c. is only used in March, April, and May.
    d. holds the boat directly to the pier at amidships.

20. **The correct anchor for your boat will depend not only on the size and type of your boat but on the:**
    a. cost (always purchase the cheapest anchor available).
    b. size and length of your anchor rode.
    c. types of seabed and amount of wind and current you expect to encounter.
    d. location (bow or stern) from which you anchor.

21. **Never anchor a boat from the stern alone because:**
    a. when windy, waves can overwhelm a small boat and enter the boat over the transom.
    b. the bow should always be pointing away from the wind.
    c. it is difficult to adjust the rode for proper scope.
    d. it is difficult to bring persons over the bow in an emergency.

22. **The ratio of the length of rode to the vertical distance (measured from the point the anchor rode is tied off on the boat to the bottom of the seabed) is called:**
    a. chock.
    b. spring.
    c. scope.
    d. wake.

23. **In normal conditions, the recommended scope of an anchor line should be approximately:**
    a. 25:1
    b. 15:1
    c. 7:1
    d. 2:1

24. **Because the Coast Guard and most states recognize personal watercraft as full-fledged boats:**
    a. operators must adhere to the same rules and regulations as larger boats.
    b. a PWC must show its navigation lights when used after dark.
    c. a PWC usually has priority of movement in meeting and crossing situations.
    d. PWCs are exempt from all boating rules and regulations.

25. Because of their different operating char acteristics, some states consider PWCs to be a special type of boat and have special regulations for them. As a PWC owner or operator you must:
    a. carry a copy of the rules of the special PWC Rules Commission aboard.
    b. know the special Navigation Rules that apply only to PWCs.
    c. follow the rules established by the National Boating Association.
    d. be aware of and abide by all laws governing the use of personal watercraft in your area.

26. Steering a PWC involves turning a movable nozzle that directs a high-pressure stream of water either right or left, turning the boat to one side or the other. It is important to know that a PWC will turn only when the:
    a. engine is turning at least 4000 rpm.
    b. jet pump is operating and pushing a stream of water.
    c. two rudders are in contact with the water.
    d. special steering pump is activated.

27. A PWC lanyard, when fastened to the emergency cut-off-switch and your wrist or PFD, will:
    a. keep your signal whistle where it can be found.
    b. alert you when you are running too fast.
    c. stop the engine when you fall off.
    d. remind you to always wear your life preserver.

28. Required equipment on a personal watercraft includes a fire extinguisher, a sound-producing device, and a:
    a. global positioning device.
    b. wearable life preserver for each person onboard.
    c. marine radiotelephone.
    d. anchor and rode.

29. When operating a PWC near shore, launch areas, swimming areas, docks, and anchored boats:
    a. take extreme care when jumping wakes in these restricted areas.
    b. run at minimum speed necessary to maintain steerageway.
    c. don't throw a wake more than three feet high.
    d. operate with the wind and current on your transom for better control.

30. If a fire occurs when operating your PWC, stop the craft immediately and:
    a. make a MAYDAY call on your VHF radio.
    b. turn on your navigation lights to attract help.
    c. leave the craft and swim as far away as possible.
    d. open the engine compartment and put out the fire.

31. Which of the following statements is TRUE?
    a. PWCs do not disturb the ecology of the water bottom.
    b. Wake from PWCs will not contribute to shoreline erosion.
    c. Noise from PWCs never disturbs bird life.
    d. As when operating any boat, having consideration for others is most important when operating a PWC.

32. It is important that a boat trailer has sufficient weight-carrying ability to:
    a. hold the boat, gear, and all passengers in it when on the road.
    b. support the boat, motor, fuel, and all gear you plan to add to it.
    c. keep the trailer on the road surface when traveling at very high speeds.
    d. carry just the weight of the boat.

33. _____ trailer tires do not track well behind the towing vehicle, but worse, will overheat, leading to blowouts.
   a. Cheap
   b. Donut-sized
   c. Over-sized
   d. Underinflated

34. Trailer winch cables and straps can snap. Be sure to:
   a. stand close by and watch the winch operation closely.
   b. tape up any winch cable that has broken strands.
   c. stay out of direct line with a winch cable or strap.
   d. release the ratchet on the winch handle.

35. Relative to the amount of trailer tongue weight, which of the following statements is TRUE?
   a. The amount of weight on the coupler ball makes no difference.
   b. Too little weight on the coupler ball will cause the trailer to fishtail.
   c. Too little weight on the coupler ball will raise the rear of the tow vehicle off the ground.
   d. You can change the weight on the coupler ball, by changing the size of the ball.

36. When launching a sailboat with the mast raised at a launch area:
   a. be careful not to tip the boat off the trailer.
   b. use a halyard to pull it off the trailer.
   c. be certain that no overhead electrical wires come close to or in contact with the mast or rigging.
   d. just as on the water, a sailboat has priority privileges.

2

What's Needed

Yes, we go boating for fun . . . but we are required to have certain safety equipment aboard. In addition, there are the Rules of the Road we must follow. To top it all off, we need to consider *doing to others as we would have them do.*

1 Operating a boat can be even more hectic and hazardous than driving a car in heavy traffic. At least on land you find directional signs, traffic control lights, lane markings, and the like. States have traffic regulations that every driver must learn. Plus, the federal government sets safety standards for roads, bridges, lights, tires, seat belts, air bags, and autobody structures. All this with the intent of preventing accidents and the injuries resulting from them.

2 Out on the water boats may be coming at you from every direction. There are no stop or yield signs and few areas where speed is regulated. Fortunately for all of us, the government has established a body of *rules of the road* for boat operators and has set some strong equipment and safety standards. It has also established a boat registration and identification system and defined some rules for law enforcement.

3 All of these regulations, collectively, are intended to prevent accidents, assure boater safety, and protect our marine environment. They are most assuredly rules you can live with. In fact, they definitely increase your odds of living.

4 This section discusses equipment, regulations, and law enforcement. We can all do our part to make boating safer by having the required equipment on board and knowing how to use and maintain it. The rules of the road will be discussed in the next chapter.

5 After completing this chapter, you should:
- Know the required equipment needed onboard your boat.
- Know about other equipment, in addition to that required by law, that can make boating safer and more pleasurable.
- Know the requirements of boat registration and/or documentation.
- Be familiar with United States Coast Guard(USCG) safety standards.
- Be informed about federal rules and regulations enforced by the Coast Guard and other law enforcement officers.
- Know that some state and local regulations are different from federal regulations.

Required Equipment

6 It is important that you have the required equipment onboard your boat and know how to use it. The following section will help you determine the equipment necessary for your kind of boat.

Life Preservers

7 Everyone who goes boating should have a wearable life jacket. Buy one that fits you and your type of boating; never try to alter one. Try it on before buying. It should be easy to adjust, put on, and remove. It should allow freedom of movement and be comfortable. Buy one that you will wear and wear it. Life jackets float, you don't.

Type I - Offshore
Adult: 22 lbs buoy-
ancy. 11 lbs
buoyancy. Turns
most users face up.

Type II - Near-shore
Adult: 15.5 lbs buoyan-
cy. Child: 11 lbs buoy-
ancy. Turns some
users face up.

Type III -
Floatation Aid
Adult: 15.5 lbs
buoyancy. Child: 11
lbs buoyancy. Users
must turn themselves
face up.

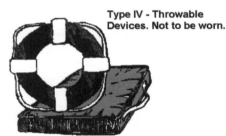

Type IV - Throwable
Devices. Not to be worn.

Type V. Special Use.
Use according to
label and outside
other clothing.

Inflatable
Devices.
Use according
to label and
outside other
clothing.

Figure 39. Life Preservers and Personal Floatation Devices

8 Coast Guard statistics show that approximately 70% of the victims in fatal boating accidents die because they end up in the water without warning or preparation. An estimated 75% of the people who drown might have been saved if they had been wearing a life jacket. Most of the victims owned life jackets but died without them. A life jacket can save your life—if you wear it.

9 **What about the 20% who *were* wearing life preservers and *still* drowned?** What happened? A significant number of victims were paddlers such as canoeists and kayakers. Paddlers have a few things working against them if they should happen to have a mishap. One, they tend to boat in remote areas far from help. Two, they often paddle alone or with just one other person. Three, their vessels are relatively unstable and easy to capsize. Paddlers are particularly at risk from entrapment. Entrapment occurs in flowing water when the boater becomes snagged on rocks or debris at a hazardous point called a *strainer*. The paddler is trapped under water because of the severe hydraulics

of the water flow and pressure. If the boater cannot escape quickly, it makes no difference what kind of life jacket is worn—the result will still be drowning.

10 **Life Preserver Requirements.** A USCG-approved, wearable life jacket [Personal Flotation Device (PFD)] is required for each person-on-board a recreational boat, including canoes, kayaks, and personal watercraft (PWC). A person being towed by the boat, such as on water skis or knee board, is considered a person on board and an approved life jacket is required either on the person or on board. A USCG Rule went into effect 23 DEC 02 requiring all children under 13 years of age to wear USCG-approved life jackets while aboard recreational vessels underway, except when children are below decks or in an enclosed cabin.

11 Life jackets must be in good condition, of appropriate size for the wearer, readily accessible, and have a legible Coast Guard approval number on the label to satisfy the requirements of a Coast Guard safety inspec-

tion. That approval means the jacket has met minimum testing standards in calm water. It is not a guarantee of its performance as a life saving device.

12 Life preservers should not be stored in a remote location, locked compartment, or under other gear. Do not store them in the plastic bags in which they were sold. (The Coast Guard does not consider that life preservers stored in their plastic bags meet the requirement of being readily accessible.)

13 On boats with cabins, life preservers need to be readily accessible from the cockpit or when on deck. On larger boats, make them available on each level of your boat. Adjust them to suit the crew members, mark them with the wearer's name, and stow them so the names can easily be read.

14 Boats over 16 feet must also carry an approved throwable device that is immediately available and ready to toss to a person in the water.

15 **Life Preserver Types.** There are five basic types of United States Coast Guard (USCG) approved life preservers.

- *Type I—Offshore Life Jackets* for all waters; especially offshore remote waters where rescue may be delayed.
- *Type II—Near-Shore Buoyant Vests* for protected waters—near shore— where fast rescue is likely.
- *Type III—Flotation Aids* for calm, protected, inland, near shore waters where there is a better chance for fast rescue.
- *Type IV—Throwable Devices* for throwing to a person in the water to grasp and hold until rescue.
- *Type V—Special Use Devices* only for special uses or conditions; label states limits of use which may include approval only when worn.

16 Types I, II, and III are the wearable life preservers of most interest to recreational boaters. The lower the number, the better

they perform. The USCG prescribed identification also provides a clue. The offshore preserver (Type I) will provide more support and protection than the near-shore equivalent life preserver (Type II). A flotation aid (Type III) provides the least security. Type I life preservers will turn most unconscious wearers face up, Type II life preservers will turn some unconscious wearers face up and Type III life preservers will not turn wearers face up.

17 Type IV life preservers are not wearable and are available only with inherently buoyant flotation. If the throwable is a cushion type device and the person in the water can put one leg through one strap and the opposite arm through the other strap with the cushion across the front of the body, there is less risk of losing the cushion while using arms and legs to maneuver.

18 Type V special use devices come in many forms from board-sailing vests, to work vests, to coverall style deck suits. The label on a Type V will indicate if it provides good support in rough water, if it will turn wearers face up, and limits of use which may include that it must be worn to meet approval requirements.

19 **Life Preservers Classes.** There are three classes of life preservers:
inherently buoyant
hybrid inflatable
inflatable

- *Inherently buoyant* life preservers are usually made with kapok or foam. Kapok is an organic fiber sealed in vinyl to prevent wetting. Foam comes in different types. Some are softer. Some are more flexible, and others are more comfortable to wear. Inherently buoyant preservers are available in all types, for adults and children, swimmers and non-swimmers. Inherently buoyant life preservers are generally lower in cost and require very little maintenance than other life preservers, but less comfortable for long periods than inflatables.

• *Hybrid Inflatable* life preservers have been available as Type V for some time but have not gained wide acceptance. They had to be worn to be considered in the carriage requirement. Recently, regulations for Types I, II and III hybrid inflatables have been issued. They do not need to be worn to meet carriage requirements. Hybrids have a small amount of inherently buoyant material but depend on an inflatable bladder for their maximum buoyancy. Models are available for children. They offer the best comfort for non-swimmers.

• *Inflatable* life jackets approved by the Coast Guard are relatively new. The regulations define Types I, II, III, and V life jackets for adults, but they are not recommended for:

• Children younger than 16 years of age
• Persons weighing less than 80 pounds
• Weak swimmers, or non-swimmers

20 Inflatable life preservers have no buoyancy until inflated. They contain an inflation cylinder that inflates the bladder either automatically or manually when you pull the lanyard. Automatic models will inflate within 5 seconds of immersion in the water. Both models can also be inflated by blowing into an inflation tube.

21 The advantage of inflatables is that they are very comfortable to wear and do not interfere with normal activity, but they cannot be worn under restrictive clothing. Automatic or accidental manual inflation could restrict breathing and injure the wearer. They are not for use in water sports where water impact is expected, such as water skiing, riding personal watercraft or white water kayaking.

22 Inflatables are available in yoke style configurations that go around the neck, with or without a safety harness; also as belt packs that are worn around the waist and pulled up over the wearer's head when inflated.

23 **Life Preserver Features.** Life preservers come in a variety of shapes, colors, and materials. Bright orange or yellow colors provide the best daytime visibility. Some have reflective strips to improve visibility at night. A small personal strobe light is also highly recommended. Staying afloat and being visible in the water is important. U. S. Coast Guard personnel wear bright orange life preservers with reflective strips. Take a lesson from them and go for visibility.

24 It is the *buoyancy* of a life preserver that keeps you afloat. It is described in pounds. In general, greater buoyancy will float you higher in the water and keep your head higher above the water. The extra lift you need varies with body fat, lung size, clothing, and whether the water is rough or calm. Test your life preserver by wearing it in the water with the clothing you expect to be wearing. It must keep your head adequately above the water and not ride up on your body.

25 Adult models of Type I inherently buoyant jackets have a minimum of 22 pounds of buoyancy, Type II and III jackets have a minimum of 15.5 pounds. Some models of hybrid jackets and inflatable jackets are the most buoyant of any life jacket available— 34 pounds. In waves, these jackets will keep your head out of the water better than any other, even when the wearer is unconscious.

26 Body heat retention varies with the style from excellent for Type V coverall style devices, to very good for Type III flotation coats, to good for some vest styles, to fair or poor for most Type I, II, and III devices.

27 **Children's Life Jackets.** Teach your children to wear a life jacket whenever they are on a boat or around the water. This is required in some states and is a USCG requirement for all children less than 13 years of age whenever aboard a boat unless below deck.or in an enclosed cabin. Children's life jackets come in child weight ranges: Less than 30 lb.; 30–50 lb.; 50–90

lb.; and over 90 lb. Because some manufacturers specify a chest size, measure your child's chest under the arms before shopping for a life jacket.

28 Children often panic and move their arms and legs violently when they fall into the water. Their life jackets must fit properly. Pick the child up by the shoulders of the jacket. If the jacket gives more than 3 inches or slips over the chin or ears, it is too large. One with a strap that goes between the legs to keep it from riding up is recommended. Buy one in a highly visible color. White is a poor choice; it looks like a white-cap in the water.

29 Test the jacket in shallow water. Children may not float face up in the water as easily as adults because their body weight is distributed differently.

30 An adult should always be with a child on or near the water. Never use a life jacket as a babysitter! Never use inflatable toys or rafts as a substitute for a life jacket. Don't leave children alone aboard a boat, regardless of the boat's size!

31 **Life Jacket Care.** Life jackets must be in good condition if they are to work correctly. Store and care for them properly. Dry them before storing. Do not crush them under heavy weights. Do not use them as cushions. Do not store them where they will be exposed to oil and grease.

32 Make regular checks for rips, tears, holes, and broken straps or hardware. Squeeze the preserver; does it feel the same as when you bought it? Kapok will become waterlogged and rot if it gets wet. Test kapok jackets by squeezing them. Can you hear air escaping through the plastic encasing the kapok? Discard those that have punctured plastic bags or show signs of waterlogging, mildew, or shrinkage.

33 Check inflatable jackets more often than inherently buoyant jackets. Check the inflation cylinder and the inflator before each outing. The cylinder should be properly installed and not punctured. The inflator has a red and green indicator that shows if it is ready for use. Red means it is not ready and should be serviced. Green means it should be ready for use. Inspect all parts for corrosion. Inflate the jacket regularly with the inflation tube checking for rips, tears, and punctures.

34 **Wear your life jacket** whenever you are on the water; you may not have time to put one on when you need it, especially if you are injured in an accident. Try putting one on in the water and you will experience the difficulty of trying to fasten it while treading water. Even strong swimmers can succumb to exhaustion or hypothermia. The extra buoyancy of a life jacket will keep you afloat, reduce heat loss, and extend survival time.

35 Everyone aboard a personal watercraft should wear a life jacket designed to withstand the impact of hitting the water at high speed. Some states require that such a life jacket be worn. Personal watercraft are designed to be ridden on, not within. You are expected to fall off. Wear life jackets with a speed impact rating suitable for the activity. Wet suits provide protection from bodily injury as well as hypothermia. They are not, however, a substitute for a life preserver unless they have a USCG approval label.

36 A person on water skies should wear a life jacket with a speed impact rating suitable for the activity. The *Impact Class* marking on the label refers to jacket strength, not personal protection.

37 Before departing, make sure all on board are wearing life preservers with straps, zippers, and ties fastened. Tuck in any loose straps to avoid having them catch on anything.

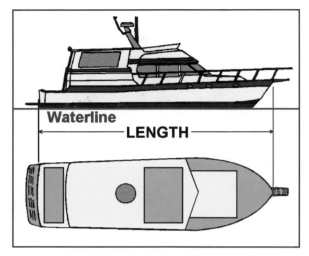

Figure 40. Measuring Boat Length

Boat Length

38 Some equipment requirements vary with the length of the boat. Measure a boat's length along its centerline from the foremost part of the hull to its aftermost part. Bowsprits, rudders aft of the transom, swim platforms, or outboard motor brackets are not included unless they are a built-in part of the hull.

Navigation Lights

39 The Navigation Rules include lighting requirements for every kind of watercraft. The requirements for navigation lights and day shapes for recreational boats less than 20 meters (65.6 feet) long are discussed in this chapter. Recognition of lights displayed by other vessels, including tugs, barges, and large vessels, is discussed in Chapter 3 and The Navigation Lights Supplement (Appendix B).

40 It is a boat owner's responsibility to equip the boat with the correct navigation lights. Display them whenever the boat is operated between sunset and sunrise or during periods of limited visibility, such as fog, rain, or haze. Lights conforming to International Rules meet the requirements of Inland Rules.

41 Lights are not provided on personal watercraft which should not be operated at night or in periods of low visibility. Many state or local regulations prohibit the use of personal water-

craft at night. If visibility is decreasing or sunset is approaching, head for home. Note: Exceptions to personal watercraft being equipped with lights include law enforcement and other official uses for a PWC. These small vessels *may* be equipped with navigation lights and flashing blue lights.

42 **Purpose of Navigation Lights.** Navigation lights serve three purposes: 1. Alert other boats of your presence and relative location. 2. Tell other boats something of your vessel's size, speed, course, and type (sail, power). 3. Enable you to properly apply the Navigation Rules.

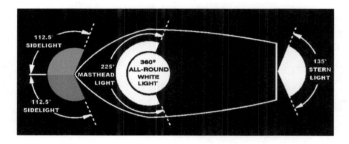

Figure 41. Navigation Light Patterns

Navigation Light Types

43

- *Masthead Lights*—white lights shining 225° forward, (112.5° on each side of the vessel) placed over the fore-and-aft centerline of a boat. Used on sailboats only when under power.

- *All-round Lights* show 360° around the horizon and may be white, red, green, or yellow, depending on their function.

- *Sidelights* are red on the port side and green on the starboard side. They shine 112.5° on each side of the vessel, from dead ahead to slightly aft of the beam.

- *Sternlights* are white lights placed at the stern that shine 135° aft (67.5° from directly astern, on each side of the vessel). If you see a sternlight you will not see the masthead light or either sidelight.

- *Towing Lights* are yellow lights having the same characteristics as sternlights and used in towing ahead, towing alongside, and pushing situations.

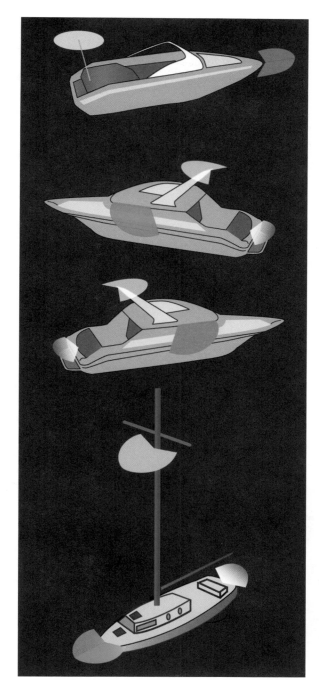

Figure 42. Navigation Lights.
Boats Less Than 12 meters (39.4 ft)
When Operating Under Power.

44 **Navigation Lights Visibility
Requirements.** Table I shows the navigation light visibility requirements for boats when underway.

Table I. Required Navigation Light Visibility		
	Vessel Length	
Light	**Less Than 39.4 ft.**	**39.4' to less than 65.6 ft.**
Masthead Light	2 miles	3 miles
All-round Light	2 miles	2 miles
Sidelights	1 mile	2 miles
Stern Light	2 miles	2 miles

45 **Navigation Light Requirements** for boats when underway are:

46 *Powerboats Less than 20 meters (65.6 ft.)* White masthead light forward, red and green sidelights (separate or combined), and white sternlight

47 *Powerboats Less than 12 meters (39.4 ft)* Masthead and stern lights may be combined into one all-round white light, with separate or combined sidelights.

48 *Sailing Vessels Less than 20 meters (65.6 ft.)* Sailboats under power display the lights of the powerboats shown in Figure 42. Sailing vessels not under power never display white masthead lights.

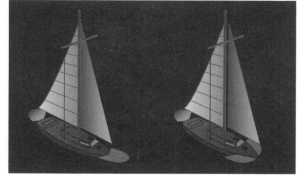

Figure 43. Navigation Lights.
Sailboat Under 20 meters (65.6 ft.)

49 The navigation lights for sailboats under 20 meters (65.6 ft.) as seen in Figure 43 include: red and green sidelights (separate or combined) plus a white sternlight.

**Figure 44.
Navigation Lights.
Sailboat Under 20
meters (65.6 ft.)
with
Masthead
Tri-Color Light**

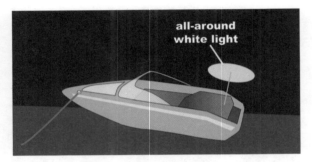

all-around
white light

Figure 46. Boat at Anchor

50 Sailing vessels less than 65.6 feet may combine sidelights and sternlights into one tri-color light at the top of the mast for better visibility when offshore as seen in Figure 44. If it is impractical for sailing vessels less than 23 feet to show the lights described above, a white light may be displayed.

when near a narrow channel, fairway, or anchorage.

Figure 45. Navigation Lights. Any vessel—sail or oars—less than 7 meters (23 ft.) must be prepared to show white light.

**Figure 47.
Day Shape
(Black Cone)
on Sailboat
More Than 12 meters (39.4 ft.)
With Sails Raised
and Under Power**

51 *Boats propelled by oars or paddles* may display the lights of sailing vessels. If this is not practicable, they may display a white electric light as shown in Figure 45 and must be prepared to show the light when conditions warrant display.

52 *Boats at anchor* must exhibit an all-round white light where it can best be seen from sunset to sunrise. However, under Inland Rules, if your boat is less than 65.6 feet long, anchor lights are not required in specially designated anchorage areas. Boats less than 23 feet long are exempt, but need to show an anchor light when in areas where other vessels normally navigate or

53 *Day shapes* are objects of specified shape and size that serve purposes similar to navigation lights during the day and are always black in color. They indicate special situations—vessels anchored (a ball), engaged in fishing (two vertical cones, points together), or sailboats operating under power with sails raised (a cone, point down). Under Inland Rules, sailboats less than 39.4 feet, operating under power with sails raised, are not required to show the day shape.

Fire Extinguishers

54   These recreational boats are required to carry fire extinguishers:

- Those with inboard engines.
- Outboard boats having closed compartments that store permanent or portable fuel tanks.
- Those with permanently installed fuel tanks. If a portable fuel tank is so heavy persons on board cannot move it, the Coast Guard considers it to be permanently installed.
- Those with closed compartments or living spaces.

Figure 48. Fire Classification Markings on Fire Extinguishers

55   **Fire Extinguishers Types.** There are three common fire extinguisher types—A, B, and C—matching the class of fire they will extinguish.

- Class A fires are in *ordinary combustible materials*, materials such as wood, paper, rubber, plastic, textiles that burn easily and can be put out with water.
- Class B fires are in *flammable liquids*, such as gasoline, oil, and grease.
- Class C fires are in *electrical equipment* such as wiring, fuse boxes, circuit breakers, machinery, and appliances.

56   **Plain water**—which is almost always available—will extinguish a class A fire. The best fire extinguisher for a recreational boat is one that will put out all three types of fires—A, B, and C. Dry chemical extinguishers are available with a rating of B–C or A–B–C. Those containing a chemical rated A–B–C are preferred. The powder blankets the fire, cutting off the oxygen that fuels the flames. It performs well under windy conditions. However, dry chemical extinguishers do leave a messy residue that you must clean up immediately to prevent corrosion.

57   There are other effective extinguishing agents such as Halon, Halon replacements, carbon dioxide, and foam. However, for various reasons these other agents do not make as good a portable fire extinguisher as do dry powder chemical agents for most recreational boats.

58   Manufacture of Halon extinguishers was halted 1 January 1994. However, if you own a Halon extinguisher, you may keep it and use it for the life of the product. Halon is a chlorofluorocarbon gas that causes damage to the ozone layer that protects the earth from excessive ultraviolet radiation. It also produces a toxic gas and you must vacate confined spaces immediately after discharging Halon.

59   At least three Halon replacements are being marketed that are more friendly to the environment. Like Halon, they leave no residue of their own. The initial offerings have been for permanent installation. One of them, FM-200, is being marketed for use in occupied areas.

60   Carbon dioxide and foam fire extinguishers are both heavy. Carbon dioxide displaces air that contains oxygen to support life, and you must vacate confined spaces immediately after discharging it. However, it is good as an engine room fire extinguisher. Foam leaves a messy residue.

61 When using portable Halon or carbon dioxide fire extinguishers in confined spaces, it is best to discharge the extinguisher from behind a partially closed door and then quickly shut the door and leave the area.

62 Purchase only extinguishers certified on the label as Coast Guard approved. Portable extinguishers should be mounted on the furnished bracket.

63 **Fire Extinguishers Sizes.** There are two sizes of Coast Guard approved extinguishers I and II. The size describes the minimum amount of extinguishing ingredient an extinguisher must hold. A size I dry chemical extinguisher must contain a minimum of 2 lb. of dry chemical. Size II must contain at least 10 lb. Therefore, a dry chemical extinguisher marked B-I would extinguish a flammable liquid fire and contain a minimum of 2 lb. of dry chemical. One marked C-II would put out an electrical fire and contain at least 10 lb. of chemical.

64 **Fire Extinguisher Requirements.** A flammable liquid fire is the most serious type of fire on a boat. For that reason, extinguishers on recreational boats must be rated for class B fires. The minimum requirements for hand portable extinguishers depend on the length of the vessel. Personal watercraft must meet the requirement for boats less than 26 ft and carry one B-I extinguisher.

Table II		
Fire Extinguisher Requirements for Recreational Vessels		
Boat Length (Feet)	**Number Req'd.**	**Type & Size**
Less than 26	1	B-I
26–<40	2	B-I
40–65	3	B-I

65 You may substitute one B-II extinguisher for two B-I extinguishers. A boat with a fixed Coast Guard approved extinguishing system in the engine room may carry one less B-I extinguisher.

66 The federal requirements listed above are minimums. The National Fire Protection Association recommends more fire extinguishers than the minimum. Equip your boat with at least one more and larger extinguisher than the minimum requirement—more and bigger, is better. A 2 lb. dry chemical B-I extinguisher will completely discharge its contents in 8 to 10 seconds!

67 **Choose the Correct Extinguisher.** You can make a fire worse by using the wrong type of extinguisher. Never use water on a class B flammable liquid fire. Oil and gasoline will float on the water and spread the fire.

68 **Know How to Use Your Extinguishers.** Remember *PASS*.
- *P*ull the safety pin.
- *A*im at the base of the fire.
- *S*queeze the handle or lever.
- *S*weep from side to side.

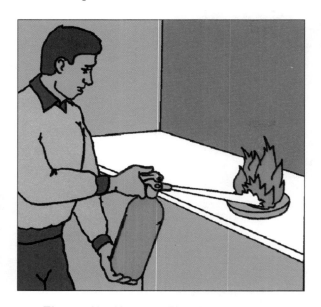

Figure 49. Using a Fire Extinguisher

69 Make sure there is a clear exit behind you and hold the unit upright. Aim the nozzle *at the base of the fire* from 6 to 8 feet away and sweep from side to side or use a series of short blasts aimed at the base. Too much

pressure from the extinguisher can cause liquids or grease to spatter and spread the fire. Watch for hot embers and repeat if flashback occurs. Many local fire departments provide practice opportunities, or you may be able to arrange one.

70 **Fire Extinguisher Location.** The key to putting out a fire is to catch it early and put it out immediately while it is still small. You must be able to get to your extinguishers quickly. Your chances are better if you have more than the minimum number of extinguishers and have them in strategic locations. Suggested locations include:

• Near the galley
• Engine compartment
• Helm
• Sleeping quarters
• The companionway
• Forward hatch.

Don't mount your extinguishers too close to fire hazards. You need to be able to get to them safely. Make sure they do not project into a busy passageway.

71 **Fire Extinguisher Maintenance.** Check the gauges on your extinguishers monthly to make sure they show a full charge. Never partially discharge extinguishers to test them; they won't be fully charged when they are needed and this may cause a leak making the extinguisher totally unusable. Always recharge or replace partially discharged extinguishers.

72 Be sure the discharge nozzle is clean; insects love to build nests inside. Slowly rock your dry chemical fire extinguisher from an upright to an upside down position several times. If you feel a thud, it means the chemical is stuck together and the extinguisher will no longer function properly. Replace it immediately and properly dispose of the old extinguisher. Check that there is no corrosion or mechanical damage to the extinguisher case.

73 Gauges may occasionally stick and be unreliable. While there is no Coast Guard requirement to inspect extinguishers annually, if your dry chemical extinguishers are the rechargeable type (metal head not plastic), you should take them to a qualified fire extinguisher service for an annual inspection to ensure they are fully charged. If they are not rechargeable, replace them or add a new one periodically. Halon type extinguishers should be weighed to ensure that the weight is equal to that stated on the label.

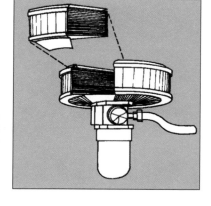

Figure 50. Flame Arrestor

Flame Arrestors

74 All gasoline engines (except outboard motors) must be equipped with an acceptable flame arrestor. A flame arrestor is the metal screen-like part that covers the carburetor air intake. It keeps flames from flashing out dangerously into the engine compartment where they could ignite gasoline fumes. Flame arrestors work by spreading and cooling the ignited fumes. They must comply with certain Underwriters' Laboratories or SAE (Society of Automotive Engineers) standards. Although flame arrestors appear to be similar to automotive air cleaners, they perform a totally different function. That is, to prevent a fire.

75 Keep your flame arrestors in good condition. There should be no holes in the grids through which flames might advance. Keep them clean. Do this not only for safety purposes but to allow your engine to operate efficiently.

Sound Producing Devices

76 The Navigation Rules require you to use sound signals in periods of restricted visibility and in meeting, crossing, and overtaking situations. Restricted visibility is visibility less than your side lights, which is 1 mile for boats less than 12 meters (39.4 feet).

**Figure 51.
Sound Producing
Devices:
Whistle,
Air or Electric Horn,
Bell,
Gas-Powered Horn.**

76 The law requires you to have some means of making an efficient sound signal. A whistle or horn, and a bell, are required on vessels 39.4 feet or more in length. For small boats and personal watercraft a plastic whistle is the simplest way to satisfy the requirement. If you request a Vessel Safety Check from either the Power Squadron or the USCG-Auxiliary you will required to have a horn or whistle that can produce a 4 second sound audible for 1/2 mile.

Visual Distress Signals

77 Electronic devices such as a VHF radio are very helpful in an emergency, but you should not depend only on electronic equipment that may go out of service. Visual distress signals will help you attract attention and get help when needed.

Visual Distress Signal Requirements.

78 Boats used on coastal waters, the Great Lakes, and those waters connected directly to them, up to a point where a body of water is less than 2 miles wide, must be equipped with Coast Guard approved visual distress signals. Boats owned in the United States, operating more than 3 miles offshore, also must be equipped with Coast Guard approved visual distress signals. They must be in serviceable condition and readily accessible. These following vessels are exempt unless they operate after dark (from sunset to sunrise):

• Recreational boats under 16 feet in length, including personal watercraft.

• Boats participating in events such as races, regattas, or marine parades.

• Open sailboats less than 26 feet, not equipped with motors.

• All manually propelled boats.

79 If you go offshore more than a half-mile or so in a small boat or personal watercraft, you should carry visual distress signals even though they are not required by federal regulation on boats less than 16 feet during daylight hours. Waving for help from that distance may not be obvious to those on shore.

Visual Distress Signal Types

80 There are two kinds of distress signals: pyrotechnic and non-pyrotechnic.

81 **Pyrotechnic devices** are similar to fireworks and include:

• Red flares—hand-held, aerial meteor, or parachute.

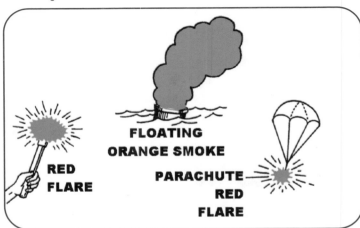

Figure 52. Pyrotechnic Visual Signals

• Orange smoke—hand-held or floating.

Pyrotechnic devices are marked with an expiration date, beyond which they will not meet requirements. However, keep those with expired dates as backup devices, for they *may* work. Small seven-second flares are minimally adequate, even though they satisfy Coast Guard requirements. *Bigger is better.*

82 Store all pyrotechnic signals in a cool, dry location in a red or orange watertight container clearly marked in large letters: **DISTRESS SIGNALS.**

83 Use pyrotechnic signals safely. They can cause personal injury and property damage if you do not handle them properly. These signals produce a very hot flame, and the residue can cause burns and ignite flammable material. For safety's sake, tape your hand-held flares to the end of a mop handle or boat hook. This will allow you to hold the burning flare away from the boat to avoid burns from dripping slag.

84 Always consider wind direction when you use a rocket-propelled distress signal. To avoid starting a fire, never fire a pyrotechnic device straight up or in such a direction that it may land in your boat, another boat, or on land. Some states classify pistol launched and hand-held aerial meteors and parachute

flares as firearms. You may be required to have a permit to legally use them.

85 Those who travel offshore should consider SOLAS (Safety Of Life At Sea) flares—they're brighter and the parachute flares burn longer and shoot to 1000 feet or more.

86 **Non-pyrotechnic** *devices* must be in serviceable condition, readily accessible, and certified by the manufacturer to comply with Coast Guard requirements.

• Orange distress flags (day signal only). Black square and ball on an orange background, at least 3 feet square.

• Electric distress lights (night use only). Must automatically flash the international distress signal—SOS (dot-dot-dot, dash-dash-dash, dot-dot-dot). Under Inland Navigation Rules, any high-intensity white light that flashes at regular intervals from 50 to 70 times per minute is a distress signal.

• Mirror (day signal only). Very effective in sunlight and requires no power.

• Dye markers (day signal only). Mostly for offshore use.

87 The international distress signal of slowly and repeatedly raising outstretched arms to each side is a simple attention getter. (Do not wave arms over the head; it looks like a greeting.)

Meeting Visual Distress Signal Requirements.

88 Three pyrotechnic devices, red flares or orange smoke, are required to satisfy the day requirement. Three pyrotechnic red flares or an electric distress light will satisfy the night requirement. The simplest solution that satisfies both the day and night use requirements is three red flares, hand-held or aerial. The following are examples of the variety and combination of devices that meet requirements:

• 3 hand-held red flares (day and night).

• 1 hand-held red flare, and two parachute

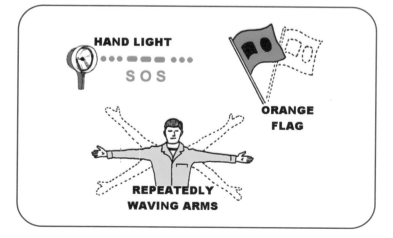

Figure 53. Non-Pyrotechnic Visual Signals

flares (day and night).

- 1 hand-held orange smoke signal, 2 floating orange smoke signals (day), and 1 electric distress signal (night only).

89 Regulations prohibit the use of visual distress signals on the water at any time except when you actually require assistance to prevent immediate or potential danger to persons on board. The Coast Guard dispatches a vessel and/or aircraft each time they receive a report of a distress signal. Unless there is immediate danger, do not fire off flares until you are sure there is a chance of an airplane or other vessel seeing them.

Additional Recommended Equipment

90 Equipment required by law is only part of that needed for safe and comfortable operation. Imagine being out in a small boat without basic necessities such as oars, paddles, anchor, rode, bailer, compass, and charts!

91 A checklist of additional equipment you may want to consider follows. Select those items that suit your boat and operating area.

Personal Watercraft (PWC)

92 **Nice to Have:**
- Goggles
- Gloves
- Footwear
- Sunscreen
- Towline

Small Boats

93 **Need to Have:**
- Anchor and rode
- Bailer/bucket
- Bilge pump (if appropriate)
- Compass
- Tools
- Charts and plotting tools
- Docking lines
- Oars or paddles
- First-aid kit and manual
- Flashlight or spotlight
- Spare parts, sheer pins (if used)
- Drinking water for emergencies

94 **Nice to Have:**
- Anchor spare
- Binoculars
- Boat hook
- Depth sounder
- Fenders
- Flash or spotlight
- Hailer or VHF radio
- Propeller spare
- Hand bearing compass
- Sunglasses
- Sunscreen
- Towline
- Motor oil, transmission fluid and grease

Large Boats

95 **Need to Have:**
- Anchor and rode
- Anchor spare
- Bilge Pump automatic
- Binoculars
- Bilge Pump high volume, manual
- Bucket (fire fighting/bailing)
- Charts/plotting tools
- Boat Hook
- Compass
- Docking lines
- Fenders
- Flashlight
- First aid kit and manual
- Radar reflector
- Food and water for emergencies
- Spare parts and batteries
- Spotlight
- Tide tables
- Tools
- VHF radio

96 **Nice to Have:**
- Clothing extra
- Emergency tiller
- Hand bearing compass
- Heaving line
- Light list
- Propeller spare
- Motor oil, transmission fluid and grease
- Sails spare
- Sea anchor
- Signalling mirror
- Sunglasses
- Sunscreen
- Swim ladder
- Towline

Boats Operating Offshore

97 **Nice to Have:**
- GPS
- Satellite EPIRB
- Immersion suits in colder waters
- Inflatable life raft

Vessels Visiting Canada

98 Vessels visiting Canada are exempt from the Canadian Shipping Act but must comply with the equipment regulations of their country of registration.

Boat Registration

99 Most vessels need to be registered in the state of principal use unless they are documented with the Coast Guard. In some states even documented boats must be registered. Any boat with a motor must be registered. Personal watercraft are classified as boats and need to be registered. Some states require vessels without motors, such as sailboats, to be registered. Check your state requirements.

Numbering

100 When you register your boat, you will receive a registration certificate that must be on board whenever the vessel is in use. Keeping it in a waterproof container will protect it from the elements.

101 **Notify the state agency** that issued your certificate within 15 days if:
- Your boat is transferred, destroyed, abandoned, lost, stolen, or recovered.
- Your certificate is lost or destroyed.
- Your address changes.

102 Attach your assigned numbers and letters permanently to each side of the forward half of your boat so that they read from left to right. If placement on a flared bow would make them difficult to read, place them on some other part of the forward half of the vessel where they can be easily read.

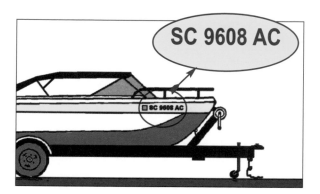

Figure 54. Typical Registration Number

103 Personal watercraft numbers and letters must be affixed on each side of the forward half of the vessel on the hull as high above the waterline as practical. If the size and shape of your personal watercraft make it difficult to apply the registration figures so they may be easily read, consult with state authorities. Use block letters at least 3 inches high in a color that contrasts well with the color of your boat. Examples would be black on white, or white on black.

104 The first two letters identify the state and are followed by a combination of numbers and letters that identify your boat. Separate the state and boat figures by a space equal to the width of any letter or numeral (except an "I" or a "1").

105 Attach state registration stickers in accordance with state instructions. Do not display any other numbers nearby.

106 Boats with a valid registration in the state of principal use can be operated in other states for limited periods of time without being registered in the latter state. If you are planning to take your boat to another state, check the time period allowed to operate there without registering your boat in that state.

Documentation

107 Documentation is an optional form of national registration for yachts of five or more net tons. (Tonnage in this case is not displacement, but carrying capacity where one ton of cargo is assumed to occupy 100 cubic feet.) Documentation eliminates concern over the legal term *state of principal use* for those who spend time in different states. It may also be more readily accepted as proof of ownership when entering foreign waters. Documentation is handled by the Coast Guard and information on the procedure can be obtained by calling (toll-free) 1-800-799-8362.

USCG Boating Safety Standards

108 A body of law enforced by the United States Coast Guard governs certain boating safety standards that domestic manufacturers and importers must observe.

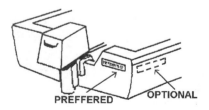

Figure 55.
Hull Identification Number Location

Hull Identification Number

109 All boats have a hull identification number (HIN) of 12 characters and may be preceded by a country-of-manufacture designation. In addition to uniquely identifying a boat, the HIN has an important safety purpose. It allows the owner to check available records to determine if this boat is one of those having any defect or being involved in a recall. An HIN number is not the same as the state registration number for display on the bow of

a boat. The HIN, however, does appear on the boat's state registration certificate. A typical HIN could be:

ABC 12345 K9 99

Read the HIN as follows:
ABC = Manufacturer or importer.
12345 = Hull serial number.
K9 = Date of certification or manufacture
   K = Month (November).
   9 = Year (1999).
99 = Boat's model year corresponding to the model's year of certification or manufacture. It is illegal to alter or remove a hull identification number. If your boat does not have a hull identification number, your state will assign one.

110 Find the HIN near the top of the outboard starboard side of the transom, or near the top outboard portion of the starboard hull near the stern. On catamarans and pontoon boats you will find it on the aft crossbeam near the starboard hull attachment.

110 Boats manufactured after 1 August 1984 have a duplicate identification number in an unexposed location somewhere inside the boat or under an item of hardware. This duplicate number aids authorities in identifying your boat if the primary identification number is damaged or removed.

Maximum Capacities Label

111 A small boat may be able to seat more people and carry more gear than is safe. Overloading a boat reduces freeboard and makes it easier for the boat to swamp or to capsize in heavy waves. This is particularly true for small open bow boats.

112 The Coast Guard safety standard on rated capacities applies to all single hull boats less than 20 feet in length manufactured after 1972, but does not apply to canoes, kayaks, inflatable boats, or sailboats. The rated capacity of the boat is on the required

```
┌─────────────────────────────────────────────┐
│  ○                                        ○  │
│          U. S. COAST GUARD                   │
│         MAXIMUM CAPACITIES                    │
│ ┌─────────────────────────────────────────┐ │
│ │ 6 PERSONS OR 800 lbs.                   │ │
│ │ 1,325 LBS. PERSONS, MOTOR, GEAR         │ │
│ │ 120 H.P. MOTOR                          │ │
│ └─────────────────────────────────────────┘ │
│  THIS BOAT COMPLIES WITH U.S. COAST GUARD    │
│  SAFETY STANDARDS IN EFFECT ON THE DATE OF   │
│  CERTIFICATION.                              │
│  MANUFACTURER:    ┌──────────────────────┐   │
│                   │ ABC MARINE, INC      │   │
│  MODEL:  ┌──────┐ │ METRO, NY USA        │   │
│          │ 2050 │ └──────────────────────┘   │
│          └──────┘                            │
│  LOAD AND H.P. CAPACITY • LEVEL FLOTATION    │
│○ COMPARTMENT VENTILATION • MANEUVERABILITY ○ │
└─────────────────────────────────────────────┘
```

Figure 56.
Typical USCG Capacity Placard

maximum capacity placard, which states the following information:

- Maximum number of persons for which the boat is rated.
- Maximum total weight of those persons.
- Maximum combined weight of persons, motor, and gear for which the boat is rated.
- Maximum horsepower of any motor used on the boat.

113 The rating for maximum number of persons is merely a guide. The most important information is the *maximum combined weight of persons, motor, and gear.* Use it as the controlling figure.

114 Excessive engine power can make a boat difficult to control. Overpowering leads to excessive speed on turns with greater risk of capsizing. It can also put too much stress on the hull. The greater the horsepower, the greater the weight of the motor. This extra weight can lead to stability problems and reduce freeboard at the stern. This increases the likelihood of following seas or wakes coming aboard over the transom.

115 Many state enforcement agencies consider operating a boat in excess of maximum

capacity ratings as negligent operation. Insurance companies often refuse to insure a boat powered with an outboard engine that exceeds the horsepower rating on the capacity label. In addition, manufacturers may refuse to honor warranty claims for boats with oversized motors.

116 The safety standard for maximum capacities described above is a federal standard. State and local governments may have additional requirements. You must comply with federal, state, and local requirements. Always check with law enforcement agencies where you operate your boat for these requirements.

Vessel Certification Label

117 Boat manufacturers affix a certification label to each boat stating that the boat complies with applicable USCG Safety Standards. It is illegal to alter or remove a certification label. It may be a separate label or combined with the maximum capacities label.

Flotation Standard

118 Trying to swim to shore from a capsized or swamped boat is not recommended. Stay with the boat if it's floating. There would be fewer drownings if boaters would stay with the boat.

119 Single hull boats less than 20 feet long must be manufactured with flotation. Inboard and I/O boats must have enough flotation to keep some portion of the boat above the surface of the water after a flooding or capsizing accident. Outboard boats must float level at or just below the surface of the water if holed or swamped, even when loaded with passengers and gear. Sailboats, canoes, kayaks, and inflatable boats are exempt from compliance with this standard. If your boat doesn't have such flotation, you may want to add some.

Ventilation Systems

120 Ventilation requirements apply to boats using gasoline as a fuel. Each engine compartment or enclosed fuel tank compartment

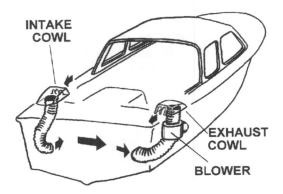

INTAKE
COWL

EXHAUST
COWL

BLOWER

Figure 57. Powered Ventilation System

must have a ventilation system which may be either a natural or a powered system.

121 A natural ventilation system consists of at least two ventilation ducts fitted with cowls. An intake duct must extend from the open atmosphere to a point midway to the bilge or below the carburetor intake in an engine compartment. An exhaust duct must extend from the lower portion of the bilge to the open atmosphere. A powered ventilation system is required on each boat compartment having a permanently installed gasoline engine with a cranking motor for remote starting.

122 A powered ventilation system consists of the system described above but with the addition of one or more powered blowers. Boats with powered systems built after 1 August 1980 will have the following label at each ignition switch.

> **Warning**
> **Gasoline vapors can explode. Before starting engine, operate blower for at least 4 minutes and check engine compartment bilge for gasoline vapors**

123 If your boat bears a label containing the words "This boat complies with U.S. Coast Guard safety standards" you can assume that the design of your boat's ventilation system meets applicable regulations. However, you are responsible for keeping the ventilation systems in operating condition.

Law Enforcement

124 Operation of any vessel within the jurisdiction of local, state or national laws carries the responsibility to obey all of those laws. Enforcement of these laws is the responsibility of the applicable officers.

Boardings

125 The Coast Guard and other federal, state, and local law enforcement officials may board your boat at any time to conduct a safety inspection. If hailed by a law enforcement vessel, follow the boarding officer's instructions. Boardings provide the Coast Guard with an opportunity to observe boaters and their equipment under actual operating conditions. The Coast Guard finds some kind of non-compliance with safety requirements in nearly half the boardings it conducts each year. Avoid penalties by following the Navigation Rules and all regulations described in this section.

Termination of Use

126 A Coast Guard boarding officer observing a boat being operated in an especially hazardous condition may direct the operator to take immediate steps to correct the condition. This may include terminating the use of the boat and returning it to port. The following are typical reasons for ordering termination of use:

• Insufficient number of Coast Guard approved life jackets.
• Insufficient number of fire extinguishers.
• Overloading beyond the manufacturer's recommended safe-loading capacity.
• Improper navigation light display.
• Inadequate ventilation systems.
• Fuel leakage.
• Fuel in the bilge.
• Improper backfire flame control.
• Operation of an unsafe vessel.

Alcohol, Drugs, and Boating

127 The use of alcohol and drugs is a significant problem on the water. Typically about 50% of all boating fatalities involve alcohol, although that percentage has dropped in some states due to public awareness and enforcement of laws regarding boating under the influence. According to federal law, you are intoxicated if your blood alcohol content is 0.10% or higher. In some states the blood alcohol standard is less than 0.10%.

128 Statistics involving accidents where the operator is under the influence of drugs are more difficult to obtain, but they are occurring. Drugs are illegal regardless of the amount of the drug present, but it's not always clear whether a drug is affecting a person's competence. Drug testing has no established threshold at which a person is considered to be legally *under the influence.* Drugs stay in the blood stream for extended periods making the evaluation of drug-related accidents difficult.

129 Alcohol and drugs affect your judgment and keep you from thinking clearly. It will take longer for your eyes, ears, and other senses to react. Alcohol also reduces your ability to survive if you fall overboard. Alcohol affects passengers in these ways as well as the boat operator. Research and experience show that 4 hours of exposure to noise, vibrations, sun, glare, wind, and other motion on the water produces *boater's fatigue.* Your reaction time is affected almost as much as if you were legally drunk. Adding alcohol increases the effect thereby increasing the risk of accidents. **Boat smart!** Don't drink or use drugs and operate a boat! A boat's captain is responsible for the conduct of all passengers on the boat. Monitor their actions and behavior at all times!

Negligent Operation

130 The Coast Guard imposes penalties for negligent operation that endangers life and property. Examples of negligent operation are:
• Operating a boat in a swimming area.
• Operating a boat while under the influence of alcohol or drugs.
• Excessive speed in the vicinity of other boats or in dangerous waters.
• Hazardous water skiing or personal watercraft practices.
• Bowriding or riding on a seatback, gunwale, or transom.

Accident Reporting

131 The majority of boat accidents are caused by the boat operator. The primary causes of accidents have been operator inattention, carelessness, and speeding. Collision with another vessel is usually the most reported type of accident.

132 Personal watercraft accidents follow the same pattern. However, the number of accidents involving personal watercraft is higher than would be expected, considering the number that are registered. Most often the collision is with another personal watercraft and most often it's not the registered owner operating the personal watercraft.

133 The message is clear—pay attention when operating a boat and make sure that anyone else operating your boat also pays attention, understands how it maneuvers, and is well versed on safe operating practices.

134 Even though we hope you will never be involved in an accident the federal regulations for reporting accidents are as shown in the following table.

Table III Accident Reporting Regulations		
Notify Authorities Immediately	File Written Report Within 48 Hours	File Written Report Within 10 Days
Fatal accidents when a person dies or disappears.	If a person dies or disappears or if there are injuries requiring more than first-aid.	Accidents involving damage more than $2000 or complete loss of a vessel.

135 Accidents involving a fatality should be reported immediately by the operator or owner of the vessel to the closest available law enforcement agency, such as the state police, sheriff, or local police. Other accidents can be reported to the State Boating Office for the state in which the accident occurred. (For a list of State Boating Offices, see Appendix C.) *All vessels* involved in an accident must file a report.

136 The following information is required:
- Date, time, exact location of the accident.
- Name of each person who died or disappeared.
- Number and name of the vessel.
- Names and addresses of the owners and operators.

Note that the above are federal regulations regarding accident reporting. The regulations of local governments may be more stringent. The safest approach is to report any type of accident as quickly as possible to the closest available law enforcement agency and to your insurance company. An example of a Boating Accident Report form is located in Appendix F.

137 You may call the U.S. Coast Guard Customer Infoline (1-800-368-5647) for additional information regarding accident reporting.

Rendering Assistance

138 The person in charge of a boat is obligated by law to provide assistance that can be safely provided to any individual in danger at sea. Failure to do so can result in a fine and/or imprisonment.

Responsibilities

139 Operating a boat carries with it certain legal and ethical responsibilities. These responsibilities include required equipment, operations and protection of the environment.

Equipment

140 When you rent a boat or personal watercraft you are the captain. You are responsible for having the required equipment on board, not the rental agency. A captain is always responsible for a boat's equipment, operation, and safety of its passengers.

Wake

141 You are responsible for damage to persons or property caused by the wake of your boat. If your boat creates a wake that rocks another boat enough to injure a person or damage the boat or equipment, you are liable for both criminal and civil actions. Anticipate wake problems. Observe the water, not just behind you, but at a distance where your wake may be hitting other boats, docks, or the shoreline. Heavy wakes striking the shore can cause serious erosion. Consider the effects of your wake on boats you meet. Slow down some distance away to reduce the effect of your stern wake.

Aquatic Nuisance Species

142 To help prevent the spread of the latest plague of non-native fish and Zebra mussels

in our waterways, boaters can follow these simple rules.

- Remove visible mud, plants, fish, or animals from boats and trailers prior to transporting them to another body of water.
- Scrape any mussels from the boat or out-drive and flush the hull, bilges, and water-holding compartments with hot (at least 120° F) water, if available.
- Do not release plants or fish, including bait, into a body of water unless they came from that same body of water.
- Pump fresh water through the engine(s) before leaving the area.
- Drain bait buckets plus the bilge, live, and transom wells.
- Remove water from trailer boats by removing drain plugs and parking on an incline to facilitate drainage.
- Use high-pressure hot water (if available) to wash both boat and trailer.
- Let boat, trailer, and equipment dry for at least five days.
- Completely drain water from any canoes, kayaks, dinghies, etc.

Apply these same rules to:
- Scuba-diving equipment.
- Waterfowl hunting gear.
- Angler's rods and equipment
- Sailboats and sailboards.
- Personal Watercraft
- Water-skiing equipment
- Seaplanes

Water Pollution

143 As a boater, you will not want to foul water that forces the closing of shellfish beds or swimming beaches, nor make people sick by depositing bacteria, viruses, or toxins in recreational waters. Federal law prohibits throwing, discharging, or depositing any refuse matter (including trash, oil, sewage, garbage or other pollutants) into the waters of the United States.

Disposal of Toxic Substances

144 Federal Law prohibits the discharge of oil or other hazardous substances into navigable waters. Oil residue may build up in the bilge and might be pumped overboard to pollute an area. This may also happen when drain plugs are removed from a boat on a lift or trailer. Take precautions to prevent this happening.

145 **Important.** *Report any oil spill* to the Coast Guard immediately. Report *any* discharge of a hazardous substance that causes a film, discoloration, or emulsion to form on or beneath the water's surface.

146 There are penalties for every discharge of a *harmful quantity of oil*. If your boat is over 26-feet long, you must post a special 5 by 8-inch placard (see Figure 58) summarizing these requirements near your engine compartment.

DISCHARGE OF OIL PROHIBITED

The Federal Water Pollution Control Act prohibits the discharge of oil or oily waste into or upon the navigable waters and contiguous zone of the United States if such discharge causes a film or sheen upon, or discoloration of, the surface of the water, or causes a sludge or emulsion beneath the surface of the water.
Violators are subject to a penalty of $5,000.

Figure 58. Oil Discharge Placard. (Shown here at reduced size. The placard must be 5 x 8-inches and posted near the engine compartment.)

Sewage Discharge

147 The law states that it is illegal to discharge raw sewage into the ocean from a vessel within 3 miles of the coastline, or in sounds, bays, navigable rivers, or the Great Lakes. Recreational boats with installed toilet facilities must have an operable Coast Guard certified marine sanitation device (MSD). These devices are of various types. Type I and II devices treat sewage with disinfectant

chemicals before discharging it into the water. Type III MSDs include recirculating and incinerating devices, and holding tanks.

148 Vessels equipped with Type I and II devices must seal their MSDs to prevent discharge when in *No Discharge Zones*. No Discharge Zones are areas of water that require greater environmental protection, and where even the discharge of treated sewage could be harmful.

149 Because of the growing number of no discharge zones and the increasing number of boaters, the federal government and the states are assisting with funding additional pumpout stations along U.S. waterways.

150 *Use your head—don't pollute.* Install a Coast Guard approved marine sanitation device in your boat, preferably one with a holding tank. Be aware of local anti-pollution laws wherever you boat.

Garbage

151 Dumping of garbage into the sea is a worldwide problem. Volunteers recently collected 1,000 tons of garbage from our seashores in just 3 hours. Sixty percent of this was plastic waste capable of killing fish and marine wildlife and fouling vessel propellers and cooling systems.

152 The law prohibits dumping garbage and plastic refuse into U.S. waters. If your boat is over 26-feet long, you must prominently post a 4 by 9-inch placard notifying passengers of dumping restrictions. A reduced size illustration of the placard is seen in Figure 59 below. The actual placard *must* be the correct 4 x 9-inch size

Waste Management Plan

153 Vessels 40 feet and longer, equipped with a galley and berthing, are required to have a written Waste Management Plan aboard. The plan must describe the procedures for collecting, processing, storing, and discharging garbage. It must designate the crewmember responsible for carrying out the plan. Remember, as the skipper, you are responsible for knowing where the plan is, explaining it to your crew, and enforcing it.

154 Do not throw anything into the water that did not come out of it. Save all of your trash and food waste, and return it to shore to recycle or dispose of properly. Boaters who witness suspected violations of boat

---

It is illegal for any vessel to dump plastic trash anywhere in the ocean or navigable waters of the United States. Annex V of the MARPOL TREATY is a new International Law for a cleaner, safer marine environment. Each violation of these requirements may result in a civil penalty up to $25,000, a fine up to $50,000, and imprisonment up to 5 years

| U.S. Lakes, Rivers, Bays, Sounds and 3 miles from shore ILLEGAL TO DUMP Plastic & Garbage Paper Metal Rags Crockery Glass Dunnage Food | 3 to 12 miles ILLEGAL TO DUMP Plastic Dunnage (lining & packing materials that float) also if not ground to less than one inch Paper Crockery Rags Metal Glass Food | 12 to 25 miles ILLEGAL TO DUMP Plastic Dunnage (lining & packing materials that float) | Outside25 miles ILLEGAL TO DUMP Plastic |

State and local regulations may further restrict the disposal of garbage.

Figure 59. Garbage Dumping Restrictions Placard (Shown reduced size, must by 4 by 9-inch size)

garbage-dumping laws should report these violations to the U. S. Coast Guard.

Environmental Summary

155 We all enjoy America's lakes, rivers and coastal waters. To keep them healthy and productive, follow good environmental boating practices as seen in the following **Top Ten Green Boating Tips.**

1. Keep your bilge clean—do not pump oily water overboard.
2. Use bilge sorbents instead of detergents.
3. Don't dump your sewage in confined waters—use a holding tank.
4. Observe local and federal sewage regulations.
5. Bring your garbage home—don't litter.
6. Use detergents sparingly—even biodegradable cleaners are hard on the aquatic environment.
7. When fueling, do not top-off tanks. Clean up any spilled fuel.
8. Use only paints approved for marine use.
9. Avoid shoreline erosion—watch your wake and propeller wash.
10. If fishing, practice *catch and release.*

State and Local Regulations

156 Boating regulations discussed in this manual are those of the federal government. State and local governments often have additional rules governing the operation of boats. In some cases states change federal rules to meet their own requirements or to further regulate boating activities within their boundaries. Some states have licensing and minimum age requirements to operate a boat or personal watercraft. Your state may require that everyone aboard a personal watercraft wear an approved life jacket. Most states require that board sailors wear life jackets. Everyone engaged in water sports should wear a life jacket with a speed impact rating suitable for the activity whether or not required by state regulation.

157 You will receive instruction in this course on local and state regulations that differ from federal regulations. If your state requests that the course examination include questions relative to their regulations, your examination will include those questions.

158 Most states provide guides that describe boating regulations in their area. Appendix C lists the name, address, and telephone number of state boating agencies where you may obtain these guides.

Noise limits

159 Some states have noise level limits on boat and personal watercraft exhaust systems. Whether your state has noise regulations or not, excessive noise not only disturbs other boaters and shoreline residents, but also birds. Do not modify your exhaust systems and don't irritate others by operating boats or personal watercraft in one area for extended periods.

Water-skiing

160 In most states, laws pertaining to water-skiing also apply to towing surfboards, tubes, discs, and kite skis. The following are some of the regulations that may apply:

- Minimum age for boat operators, water skiers, and observers.
- Wearing approved life jackets.
- An observer on every tow boat who may be required to wave a flag when the skier or the tow line are in the water.
- Time of day when you may water-ski.
- Maximum speeds of boats in near-shore areas
- Restrictions on riding inner tubes, parasailing, ski jumping, or skiing slalom course
- The use of self-propelled water skis and surfboards, or remote-controlled devices that tow water skiers

Boater Services

USPS

161 Supplemental educational material may be ordered through the toll free USPS customer service phone number 1-888-FOR-USPS (367-8777) and at many marina supply stores. A series of short courses, most designed for home study, are available covering a wide range of topics. The courses are listed on the inside of the back cover of this manual. The *United States Power Squadrons Boating Course* video, an 80 minute video tape with book that covers the boating course topics is also available.

162 For those with Internet access, additional information about USPS, services, products, and local squadrons can be obtained from the award winning World Wide Web site: **http://www.usps.org.**

163 Local Power Squadrons offer courses to members taught by experienced member instructors. Topics range from basic seamanship through celestial navigation and are described on the inside of the front cover.

USCG Customer Infoline

164 USCG Infoline operators provide callers with information on boating safety recalls and take consumer complaints about possible safety defects. They answer questions about topics such as safety equipment requirements, boating safety classes, how to register a boat, how to complete an accident report, and how to get a commercial license. They will also respond to requests for printed safety material. The Coast Guard offers a guide *Federal Requirements and Safety Tips for Recreational Boats.*

165 In the United States (including Alaska, Hawaii, Puerto Rico, and the Virgin Islands) call 1-800-368-5647 (1-800-689-0816 for the hearing impaired.) Hours are 8:00 A.M. to 4:00 P.M. Eastern Time, Monday through Friday, excepting federal holidays.

166 The district offices of the United States Coast Guard listed in Appendix D are also a source of information on federal regulations.

Figure 60. Vessel Safety Check Decal

Vessel Safety Check Program

167 The United States Power Squadrons and the U.S. Coast Guard Auxiliary conduct free Vessel Safety Checks (VSC) of pleasure boats. This program of checking and discussing safety equipment aboard your boat is designed to make boating activities safer for you, your family, friends and fellow boaters. No report about your boat is ever made to any law enforcement agency. If your boat meets the VSC Program requirements, the award of a VSC decal is your assurance that your boat is properly equipped and meets the minimum Federal Equipment Requirements. A properly equipped boat is a safer boat. The VSC program is an *annual* program. Have your boat checked every year.

What's Needed • Review

Name . . . . Date . . . . Group No. . . . .

1. **In addition to federal regulations described in this course, you must be familiar with:**
   a. the Federal Boat Safety Act of 1764.
   b. state and local regulations.
   c. laws of the Underwriter's Laboratories, Inc.
   d. liability insurance regulations.

2. **Regulations require that all recreational boats have:**
   a. USCG-approved wearable life preserver for each person on board.
   b. an anchor and rode to securely anchor the vessel under any conditions.
   c. a compass, charts, dock lines, and fenders.
   d. a radiotelephone.

3. **The wearable life preserver providing the most support and protection is a:**
   a. Type V (Special Use Device).
   b. Type IV (Throwable Device).
   c. Type I (Offshore Life Jacket).
   d. Type III (Flotation Aid).

4. **Navigation lights required on powerboats less than 65.6 feet are the same as those for sailing vessels except that a _____ is required on powerboats.**
   a. yellow all-round light
   b. red strobe light
   c. white masthead light
   d. flashing blue light

5. **Navigation lights most frequently found on sailing vessels under 65.6 feet include a white sternlight and:**
   a. red and green sidelights.
   b. a white masthead light.
   c. a blue anchor light.
   d. a yellow sternlight.

6. **The best fire extinguisher for a recreational boat is one that is Coast Guard-approved and that will put out:**
   a. halon fires.
   b. A and C fires.
   c. A, B, and C fires.
   d. carbon dioxide fires.

7. **Fire extinguishers should be mounted in strategic locations. Recommended locations are near the galley, engine compartment, helm, and:**
   a. flying bridge.
   b. sleeping quarters.
   c. anchor storage locker.
   d. head.

8. **In addition to keeping your flame arrestor free of damage, it is important to:**
   a. grease it regularly.
   b. install a new element periodically.
   c. replace the screening annually.
   d. keep it clean.

9. **Visual distress signals:**
   a. are useful only at night.
   b. are not dangerous to handle.
   c. help you attract attention and get help when needed.
   d. last indefinitely if you do not use them.

10. **Vessel equipment required by law:**
    a. is only part of that needed for safe and comfortable operation.
    b. covers all of your needs for the safe operation of your vessel.
    c. includes charts and other navigational equipment.
    d. does not include visual distress signals and fire extinguishers.

11. **Your boat has a yellow hull. After registering it with the state and receiving a boat number, you purchase:**
    a. a black plastic plate with 2 inch script letters and numbers to hang over the side.
    b. 3 inch black vertical block letters and numerals for both sides of the forward hull.
    c. lighter yellow letters and numbers for both sides of the forward hull.
    d. light gray 2-1/2 inch italic letters and numbers for the starboard upper transom.

12. **A hull identification number not only identifies your boat but:**
    a. is the registration number on the forward part of the hull.
    b. prescribes the maximum horsepower engine for which the boat is rated.
    c. identifies the materials of construction of that boat.
    d. allows the owner to check and see if this boat is one that has a defect or is involved in a recall.

13. **The most important information on a boat's Maximum Capacities Label is the:**
    a. boat's registration number.
    b. seating capacity of the boat.
    c. maximum total weight of occupants of the boat.
    d. maximum combined weight of persons, motor, and gear.

14. **A condition that could result in the termination of the use of your boat is:**
    a. the display of navigation lights in daylight.
    b. running with your fenders hanging from the sides of your boat.
    c. overloading beyond the manufacturer's recommended safe loading capacity.
    d. failure to carry charts of your cruising area.

15. **What condition affects a person's judgment, keeps the person from thinking clearly, reduces a boater's ability to survive in the water, and accounts for 50% of all boating fatalities?**
    a. indigestion.
    b. seasickness.
    c. heat exhaustion.
    d. the use of alcohol and drugs.

16. **The condition that slows reaction time after several hours on the water almost as much as if you were legally drunk is called:**
    a. hypothermia.
    b. saint vitus dance.
    c. sea leg fever.
    d. boater's fatigue.

17. **If involved in a boating accident, all operators should:**
    a. file a written report within 90 days of any accident involving damage in excess of $3000.
    b. file an accident report with the local Motor Vehicle Department within 30 days.
    c. notify the Coast Guard Auxiliary immediately if your boat sinks or anyone needs first aid.
    d. report all accidents involving death, disappearance, or serious injury of a person, or property damage over the state or federal level.

18. **The skipper of a boat is obligated by law to provide assistance to any individual in danger at sea providing that the:**
    a. recipient is adequately insured.
    b. assistance can be provided safely without endangering his own boat or crew.
    c. person in need agrees to financial remuneration.
    d. assistance cannot be provided by someone else.

19. **When you rent a boat, the person responsible for having all legally required equipment aboard is the:**
    a. dock hand who turns the boat over to you.
    b. boat's manufacturer.
    c. person who rents the boat; you.
    d. rental agent.

20. **Federal law prohibits:**
    a. depositing garbage at a marina or on shore.
    b. using a marine sanitation device that utilizes disinfecting chemicals.
    c. using incinerating marine sanitation devices.
    d. throwing, discharging, or depositing oil, garbage, sewage, or other pollutants into U.S. waters.

3

Rules to Live By

Just as there are rules by operating motor vehicles, there are several rules we *must* observe when we go boating. The primary purpose of these marine rules is to avoid accidents. Following the rules is easy—when we know them.

1   This third chapter of Boat Smart covers four major areas of safe boating:
1. Aids to Navigation—the road signs of our waters.
2. Navigation Rules—the driving laws for boaters.
3. Adverse Conditions and Emergencies—some facts and hints for coping with unexpected and unpleasant developments while afloat.
4. Marine Radiotelephone.

Aids to Navigation

2   For boaters, aids to navigation are like street signs and caution signs for drivers. Each gives you information needed to know to locate and move your vehicle (boat or car) safely.

3   We define an *aid to navigation* as any object external to the boat that:
1. Warns a boater of danger.
2. Aids a boater in finding position.
3. Helps a boater pilot a boat safely.

4   There are several distinct systems of aids to navigation used in our waters. The U.S. Aids to Navigation System marks the federal waters of the United States and is maintained by the U.S. Coast Guard. *Federal waters* include all lakes and waterways that connect with the high seas and are navigable by seagoing boats. The U.S. system is designed for use with nau-

tical charts. You can tell the exact meaning of an aid to navigation by looking at a chart. The aid also tells you where you are. Many privately maintained aids conform to the federal system.

5   Many states use the Uniform State Waterway Marking System. It differs in several ways from the U.S. System. After the review questions to this chapter you will find four color plates showing the U. S. Aids to Navigation and Uniform State Waterway Marking systems.

Marks

6   We begin our study with *marks*—aids to navigation that you see while boating. There are three classes of marks:
- *Side-of-Channel* marks identify the port and starboard sides of a route.
- *Isolated Danger* marks are placed on, above, or near a danger.
- *Special* marks call attention to a special feature of an area.

7   You can identify marks in daylight by their shape, color, markings, and sounds, and at night by their light and sound characteristics. The *U.S. Coast Guard Light Lists* describe all lights, buoys, and beacons maintained in the navigable waters of the United States.

8   Identify aids to navigation on your chart as you see them. Always use a current chart when boating; it is a necessary tool for safe

navigation. When you notice a defective or missing aid, report it to the Coast Guard.

9 **Types of Marks.** Two types of marks are used in each of the three classes of marks described above. They are called *buoys* and *beacons.*

10 **Buoys** are floating objects anchored at specific locations. They may range in size from 3 to 40 (or more) feet tall. You may identify them by their shape, color, numbers, letters, sound devices, or lights. (See color plates at the end of this chapter.) Many are built to provide a strong return signal to a boat's radar signal. This makes them useful even in times of very limited visibility.

11 Buoys appear on charts as diamonds with small circles that indicate their approximate position. Severe storms, ice, and collisions with large vessels often move buoys. Also, buoys will swing around their moorings with wind and current.

12 Lighted buoys on charts are shown by a purplish-red (magenta) outline around their position circles.

13 **Beacons** are marks that are permanently fixed (fastened) to the earth's surface. They should not move from their charted positions. They may be as large as lighthouses and as small as daybeacons. *Daybeacons* are fixed structures such as posts and pilings that are usually found in shallow water or on shore. Daybeacons support *daymarks*— boards of various shapes and colors that identify daybeacons in daytime.

14 Unlighted beacons appear on charts as small triangles or squares. Lighted beacons, called *lights*, appear on charts with purplish-red (magenta) flares which resemble exclamation marks (see color plates).

15 *Do not pass too close to beacons. You may collide with their foundations or with the very obstruction that they mark.*

16 **Shapes and Colors of Marks.** The shapes and colors of marks make it easy to identify them (see the color plates following the last page of this chapter's review questions).

17 *Conical-shaped* nun buoys and triangular-shaped daymarks show the starboard (right) side of a channel when coming in from sea— see "Red-Right-Returning" that follows. They can be either solid red or painted with red and green bands; the top band is always red.

18 *Cylindrical-shaped* can buoys and daymarks that are square-shaped show the port (left) side of a channel when coming in from sea. They can be either solid green or painted with green and red bands with the top band always green.

19 *Spherical (globe-shaped)* buoys are used for special purposes.

20 **Red—Right—Returning.** This is the **3R** Rule of the U.S. Aids to Navigation System. The rule states: *"When returning from sea, keep red side-of-channel marks to your right-hand or starboard side."* This also means that you will keep green side-of-channel marks to your left-hand or port side (see color plate 2 that follows the last page of this chapter's review questions).

21 *Returning* is defined as:
• Entering a harbor or bay from the open ocean.
• Traveling up a river from the sea, for example, up the Mississippi River from the Gulf of Mexico.
• Traveling in a clockwise direction around a land mass, for example, southerly along the Atlantic Coast or northerly along the Pacific Coast to Alaska.

22 On the Great Lakes, colors and numbering of marks start at the outlet end of each lake and proceed westerly and northerly toward their upper ends, except for Lake Michi-

gan, where the direction of these marks is southerly.

23 **Numbers and Letters.** Numbers and letters identify many marks and help you find them on charts. In the U.S. system, most solid red and solid green aids are numbered. Red marks (on the starboard side of a channel when you are returning) have even numbers; green marks (on the port side), if numbered, have odd numbers. The numbers increase in value as you return from sea, but may restart at a junction, etc.

24 **Lighted Marks.** Lighted marks help to guide you at night and during times of limited visibility. Most lighted buoys are metal floats with a light at the top of a short skeleton tower that supports the lighting mechanism. (See color plates following this chapter.)

25 The lights of marks that show the starboard side of a channel when returning from sea are red. Those that show the port side when returning from sea are green. Safe water and isolated danger buoys have white lights. Special purpose buoys have yellow lights. No other colors are used.

26 Lights on navigational aids have many patterns. As examples, *fixed pattern lights* show steadily and continuously; *rhythmic pattern lights* blink on and off with a regular pattern. Lighted aids are not always reliable, for at times their lighting mechanisms may fail. If you find a light not working after dark, notify the Coast Guard so that other boaters may be notified and the lights repaired.

The Lateral System

27 Color Plate 1 (the first of the four color plates that follow the last page of this chapter's review questions) pictures the lateral system of the U.S. Aids to Navigation System. This color plate includes side-of-channel marks, preferred channel marks, and safe water marks.

28 **Side-of-Channel Marks.** These marks identify the port and starboard sides of a channel, following the "Red-Right-Returning" rule described above. Coming from sea, port side marks on your left side will be green; starboard side marks on your right side will be red.

Table IV Side-of-Channel Marks Returning From Sea		
	Port	**Starboard**
Color	Green	Red
Shapes: **Unlighted** **Lighted**	Cylindrical (can) Skeleton Tower	Conical (nun) Skeleton Tower
Daymark	Green square	Red Triangle
Light (If fitted) Color Rhythm	Green Varied flashing	Red Varied flashing
Identification	Odd numbers	Even numbers

29 **Preferred Channel Marks.** These marks identify channel junctions and obstructions. They have red and green horizontal bands. The color of the top band indicates the preferred or major channel, in reference to the Red-Right-Returning system or going upstream. If the top band is red, the preferred channel is to the left, and you will pass the mark on your starboard side when returning.

Table V Preferred Channel Marks Returning from Sea		
	Preferred Channel to Starboard	Preferred Channel to Port
Color	Green and Red horizontal bands, top band Green	Red and Green horizontal bands, top band Red
Shapes: Unlighted Lighted	Cylinder (can) Skeleton tower	Cone (nun) Skeleton tower
Topmark (If fitted)	Green cylinder	Red cone, point up
Daymark	Green bordered square Lower enclosed portion Red	Red bordered triangle Lower enclosed portion Green
Light (If fitted) Color Rhythm	Green Flashing 2+1 (2 short flashes followed by 1 short)	Red Flashing 2+1 (2 short flashes followed by 1 short)
Identification	Letters	Letters

30 **Safe Water Marks.** These marks have safe water on both sides and identify the centers of navigable channels and off-shore approach points.

Table VI Safe Water Marks	
Color	Red & White Vertically striped
Shapes Unlighted Lighted	Spherical Skeleton tower
Topmark (If fitted)	Red Sphere
Daymark	Octagonal red & white Divided vertically
Light (If fitted) Color Rhythm	White Morse "A" (short flash-long flash)
Identification	Letters

Non-Lateral Marks

31 In addition to the Lateral System marks described above, several other navigation aids are used by boaters. These include ranges, danger marks and special marks.

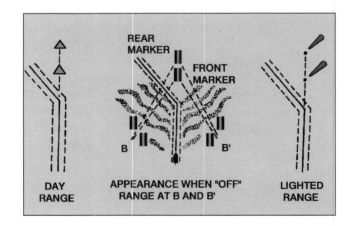

Figure 61. Typical Ranges

32 **Ranges.** Ranges are beacons used to show the centerline of a channel. They are almost always lighted. You will find two beacons placed a suitable distance apart, with the rear

beacon taller than the front beacon. When the beacons appear in a line, a boater is on a safe course in the marked channel. Any horizontal separation of the two beacons alerts a boater to steer back into the center of the channel until the two beacons are in line again. Always refer to a chart to determine what portion of a range you may travel safely.

33 Range daymarks are painted in many colors. Paired daymarks are always painted with the same colors. Letter markings often distinguish one range from another. When a range is lighted, the far light has a longer rhythm than the near light. A front range is one observed ahead of your boat; a back range is one observed astern.

Table VII Isolated Danger Marks	
Color	**Black & Red Horizontally banded Top band is black**
Shape	**Skeleton tower**
Topmark/Daymark	**Two black spheres**
Light (If fitted) Color Rhythm	**White Flashing, groups of 2**
Identification	**Letters**

34 **Isolated Danger Marks** are placed on, above, or near a danger that has navigable water all around it. Approach them cautiously. (See the first color plate that follows this chapter's review questions for examples of isolated danger marks.)

35 **Special Marks** call attention to a special feature of an area. Their meanings are described on charts, or in *Light Lists*, *Coast Pilots*, or *Local Notices to Mariners*. Examples are anchorage areas, fish nets, spoil areas, pipelines, and traffic separation schemes. (See the color plates that follow the last page of this chapter's review questions for examples of these special marks.)

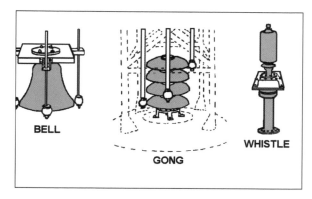

Figure 62. Sound Signals

36 **Sound Signals** on some marks help boaters find them when visibility is reduced.
- *Bells* and *gongs* produce irregular sounds from the motion of the waves. Gongs sound a variety of tones, different from bells that have a single tone.
- *Whistles* create a high-pitched sound produced by the motion of the waves. Electrically-operated *horns* give off lower-pitched sounds. You will usually find horns in areas where there is little sea motion.

Uniform State Waterway Marking System

37 The Uniform State Waterway Marking System (USWMS) was originally intended for state use on inland lakes and waterways not shown on nautical charts. It is now used on other waters and supplements the federal system.

38 **USWMS Cardinal System.** (Refer to the fourth color plate in the group following the last page of this chapter's review questions. At the bottom of this plate we see the markers for the USWMS Cardinal System.). This system is used on lakes where the idea of *returning from sea* does not apply. While many boaters will never see this limited buoyage system in use, others will. Three types of buoys mark safe passage areas. All may have lights and/or reflectors for night navigation.

39 USWMS Cardinal Buoy Codes

- A white buoy with a red top represents an obstruction. Pass to the south or west. It may have a number.
- A white buoy with a black top represents an obstruction. Pass to the north or east. It may have a number.
- A red and white vertically striped buoy indicates that an obstruction exists between the buoy and the nearest shore. (Note that this aid has an entirely different meaning from the red and white vertically striped one in the federal system.)

40 **USWMS Lateral System** outlines the edges of channels. Side-of-channel marks are solid red and black, instead of solid red and green as in the U.S. system.

41 **USWMS Regulatory Marks** marks show controlled areas, areas of danger, and exclusion areas where boats are not allowed. They are also shown in the lower left hand portion of the color plate described above.

- Regulatory marks, whether daymarks or buoys, are white. You will find orange bands around the edges of daymarks and the tops and bottoms of buoys. There is normally information on these marks that you will need to read. Slow down and proceed cautiously until you have been able to read and understand the message.
- Orange diamonds are *Dangerous Area Marks* with the word DANGER (or a description of the danger) in black letters within the diamond.
- Orange circles are *Controlled Area Marks* with the type of control indicated in black letters within the circle. Examples are "No Wake," "Slow Speed," "No Anchoring," and "Steerage Speed Only."
- Orange diamonds with a cross through them are *Exclusion Area Marks*. You may find an explanation in black letters outside the diamond. Exclusion areas

are found near dams, rapids, or swimming areas.
- Orange squares or rectangles are *General Information Marks*. Directions/information are in the center.

42 **Mooring Buoys**. Recreational boaters may tie up to mooring buoys. They are white buoys with a horizontal blue band midway between the waterline and the top of the buoy. If lighted, this buoy will show a slow flashing white light.

U.S. System Variations

43 Boaters in certain parts of the United States will encounter special navigational aids systems that differ from the United States Aids to Navigation System described above. Most notable are the Intracoastal Waterway System shown in the first of the four color plates following this chapter's review questions. The Western River System used on the Mississippi River and its tributaries are shown in the fourth color plate.

Navigation Rules

44 When driving any vehicle on public roads you must observe traffic rules to avoid accidents. Every time a boat comes near another there is a risk of collision. The Navigation Rules are traffic rules for boats, intended to prevent collisions. They prescribe how to operate a boat in the presence of other vessels and how to inform them of your intentions. Other boaters have a legal right to expect that you will operate by certain common rules.

45 The Navigation Rules apply whether you operate a 10-foot personal watercraft, a 60-foot yacht, or an oceangoing freighter. You are expected to learn and understand them in general terms. You are not expected to memorize all of the Navigation Rules or to be able to quote them word for word. Both civil and criminal penalties may be assessed for violation of these rules.

Two Sets of Navigation Rules

46 Boaters in the United States operate their vessels under two similar sets of navigation rules: International and Inland. International Rules apply to all vessels on the high seas outside established *navigational lines of demarcation.* These lines are prominently marked on coast and harbor charts with magenta (purple) dashed lines. You will find International Waters even within the continental boundaries of the United States.

47 **Inland Navigation Rules** apply on waters of the United States inside the navigational demarcation lines. Just as states have general traffic codes and special regulations for local conditions, there are Inland Navigation Rules for busy harbors, rivers, lakes, and crowded waterways.

48 If you operate a boat over 39.4 feet (12 meters) in length, you must have a copy of the Inland Navigational Rules aboard. You may purchase the booklet, *Navigation Rules, International—Inland*, from the Superintendent of Documents, United States Government Printing Office, Washington DC 20402 (202-512-1800); stock number is 050-012-00407-2. It is also available in many marine stores or federal book stores located in many cities. (This is the booklet commonly called COLREGS, or *The International Regulations for Preventing Collisions at Sea.*)

49 The International Rules and Inland Rules are similar but with some important differences. We present them in this manual as one, pointing out some significant differences.

General Rule of Responsibility

50 You, as a skipper, are responsible for complying with the Navigation Rules. However, since rules may not cover every possible risk of collision, the General Rule of Responsibility exists.

51 This rule states that nothing in the Navigation Rules frees any vessel or its owner, master, or crew, from the consequences of neglecting to comply with the rules. The skipper is not the only one responsible for error—if you are operating the boat, you must comply with the rules, or you will be held responsible.

52 Further, the General Rule requires the owner, master, or crew to use *"any precaution required by the ordinary practice of seamen, or by the special circumstance of the case."* It requires the owner, captain, and crew of a vessel to take every precaution required by the ordinary practice of good seamanship to avoid immediate danger including, and especially, collision. Another way of expressing this is that no boat has the right-of-way *through* another boat.

53 You must be alert at all times. If you are the stand-on vessel, and it appears that the other vessel is not taking appropriate action to give way, stay out of his way. There may be a reason that is not apparent to you why the give-way vessel cannot stay clear of you.

54 In interpreting and acting in accordance with the rules, *"due regard shall be had to all dangers of navigation and collision and to any special circumstances...which may make a departure from these Rules necessary to avoid immediate danger."* In other words, *common sense must prevail, even if it means breaking the rules to avoid danger.*

Definitions

55 Because the Navigation Rules contain very specific and technical language, it is important to define some of the basic terms necessary to understand them.

56 **Risk of Collision.** The skipper and crew of every vessel must use all available means appropriate to the prevailing conditions to determine if risk of collision exists. If you have *any* doubt, then the risk of collision

exists and you must take whatever evasive action is necessary to avoid collision.

57 **Sailing Vessel.** A vessel under sail only. When a sailing vessel has its engine running and the propeller engaged, it becomes a power-driven vessel, and must abide by the rules for power-driven vessels, even if its sails are raised.

58 **Power-Driven Vessel.** Any vessel propelled by machinery.

59 **Give-Way Vessel.** A vessel that must stay out of another vessel's way and take early and substantial action to do so by altering course and/or speed.

60 **Stand-On Vessel** is the term from the Navigation Rules describing a vessel that continues in the same direction and speed during a crossing or overtaking situation, unless a collision appears imminent. If the other vessel does not take appropriate action, the stand-on vessel must take whatever action is necessary to avoid collision.

61 **Underway.** A vessel that is afloat and not at anchor, aground, or made fast to shore. It is not necessarily making way (moving) through the water.

62 **Vessel Not Under Command.** A vessel unable to maneuver or keep out of the way of other vessels due to special circumstances such as engine or equipment failure. Examples are being adrift without operable power, inability to steer, and being aground.

63 **Vessel Restricted in Ability to Maneuver.** A vessel unable to keep out of the way of other vessels due to the nature of its work. Maneuvering may be difficult as in towing, dredging, and diving.

64 **Vessel Engaged in Fishing.** A vessel restricted in maneuverability as a result of nets, lines, or trawls. A vessel which is trolling is not restricted in maneuverability. Recreational vessels trolling lines have no special rights or privileges.

65 **Restricted Visibility.** A condition when vessels are unable to see each other because of fog, haze, mist, rain, sleet, snow, high seas, etc.

66 **Whistle.** Any sound signaling device (including a horn) capable of producing a prescribed blast.

Sound Signals

67 Sound signals are important methods of communicating with other vessels. Under Inland Rules, specified *maneuvering and warning signals* are sounded to announce a skipper's intentions to other vessels and to gain their agreement to those maneuvers.

- **Short blast.** Blast of about 1 second duration.
- **Prolonged blast.** Blast of 4-6 seconds duration.

68 **Restricted visibility signals** are used to warn nearby vessels of another vessel's presence. It is important that skippers be familiar with signals designated for use in restricted visibility, so that the type and size of vessels encountered may be recognized.

69 **Maneuvering and Warning Signals** are used most often by powerboats in three dangerous close-approach situations—*meeting, overtaking,* and *crossing.* However, sailing vessels (not under power) must also use them in overtaking situations, and they may exchange them with other sailing vessels. These signals are not used until vessels are in sight of one another.

70 If the other vessel agrees with your maneuver, it returns the same signal. It should never use cross signals. For example, returning two blasts for one blast. Instead, if it does not agree, it sounds the danger signal. That is, five or more short and rapid blasts on the whistle.

Table VIII Maneuvering and Warning Signals	
Meaning	**Number of Blasts**
"I intend to turn to my right and pass you on my PORT side."	1 Short
"I intend to turn to my left and pass you on my STARBOARD side."	2 Short
"I am operating with ASTERN propulsion. "My engine is in reverse."	3 Short
"I am DEPARTING from a dock, pier, or mooring." "I am APPROACHING a channel bend or intervening obstruction."	1 Prolonged
"There is DANGER in what you intend to do!" "I am in doubt as to your intentions." "I do not agree with your intended maneuver."	5 or more Short

Table IX Restricted Visibility Signals	
Vessels At Anchor in Restricted Visibility	
Length of Vessel	**Signal Required**
Vessels under 39.4 feet (12 m) in length	A bell is not required. Any efficient signal device may be sounded every 2 minutes.
Vessels 39.4 feet and less than 328.1 feet (100 m) in length	Ring a bell rapidly for 5 seconds of every minute
Vessels 328.1 feet or more in length	Ring a bell rapidly for 5 sec. in the forepart of the vessel, followed by ringing a gong 5 sec. in the after part
All vessels	May supplement bell ringing with 3 whistle blasts in succession. One short, one prolonged, one short.
Vessels under 65.6 feet (20m)	Not required to sound sound signals if anchored in a special anchorage area.
Vessels Underway in Restricted Visibility	
Type of Vessel	**Number of Blasts**
Powerboats making way	**1 prolonged blast every 2 minutes**
Powerboats underway but stopped	**2 prolonged blasts every 2 minutes**
Sailing vessels. Vessels restricted in ability to maneuver. Vessels not under command.	**1 prolonged blast followed by 2 short blasts every 2 minutes**

Pay attention if you hear a danger signal—*you* may be the one in danger. Never proceed until the situation is clear. Whenever you make a course change, always make it obvious.

71 In inland waters sound signals (or radiotelephone messages) *must* be exchanged about close-approach situations.

72 There is an important difference when boating in international waters. Here a signal given indicates that the maneuver *is being carried out*, rather than merely *intended* (as in inland waters). Return signals are given only in overtaking situations in narrow channels or fairways, or where necessary when approaching other vessels.

73 **Restricted Visibility Signals.** You must sound the proper sound signal for your type of boat and circumstance whenever anchored or underway in restricted visibility.

74 **Sound Signal Requirements.** Boats under 39.4 feet (12 meters) including personal watercraft may use any sound producing mechanism that makes an efficient sound. Canister horns are good for this purpose, but even a police or similar whistle may be used.

75 Boats 39.4 feet (12 meters) or more must be equipped with a whistle and a bell audible for at least *one nautical mile.* State regulations may differ.

76 Vessels over 328.1 feet (100meters) have additional requirements.

Steering and Sailing Rules

77 The steering and sailing rules are general rules of navigation directed at the conduct of vessels in three general situations:
- Vessels in any condition of visibility;
- Vessels in sight of one another;
- Vessels in restricted visibility.

78 **Vessels In Any Condition of Visibility.** Various approved Rules of the Road apply in differing situations faced by the boater in differing visibility conditions. Familiarity with these rules could save your boat and life.

Table X Vessel Priority	
Vessel Status	**Example**
1 Not Under Command	No steerage No power
2 Restricted in Ability to Maneuver	Underwater operations, surveying, dredging
3 Constrained by Draft	Deep draft vessel in narrow channel
4 Fishing or Trawling	Using lines, nets or trawls. (not trolling)
5 Sailing	Under sail, no power
6 Power-Driven	Last in ranking

79 **Vessel Priority.** Except in overtaking situations and narrow channels, where specifically required otherwise, there is an order of priority for vessels. The further down the table, the less priority the vessel has. Notice where simple sailboats and powerboats are listed.

80 **Lookout.** Coast Guard statistics show the major cause of collisions is improper lookout. When under way, you are required to maintain a lookout at all times. Be alert for the sight and sounds of other boats. A proper lookout is a major factor in preventing collisions.

81 **Safe Speed.** You are required to proceed at a safe speed at all times. Safe speed is a speed that allows you to stop your boat in time to avoid collision. Visibility, wind and sea conditions, depth of water, the amount of vessel traffic, the ability of a boat to maneuver, and the proximity of navigational hazards are all factors entering into the determination of safe speed. Local and state regulations may regulate the speed of your boat more specifically, even in open waters.

82 **Narrow Channels.** Vessels proceeding in a narrow channel or fairway must keep as near to the outer limit of the channel that lies to their starboard side as is safe and practicable. Vessels must not impede the passage of larger vessels and vessels that can safely navigate only within a narrow channel and they must never cross in front of these vessels. Fishing or anchoring in a narrow channel should be avoided. Narrow channels should be crossed at right angles to the centerline of the channel to minimize interference with other vessels.

83 **Rounding a Bend.** Be alert and proceed with caution when nearing a bend in a channel where you cannot see vessels approaching from the other direction. Sound one prolonged blast of your whistle. Any vessel within hearing should answer in kind.

Vessels in Sight of One Another

84 Steering and sailing rules for three close-approach situations that could involve collision—overtaking, meeting, and crossing.

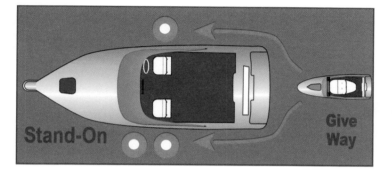

**Figure 63. All Overtaking Vessels.
One Blast (⊙) When Passing to Right of Overtaken Vessel.
Two Blasts (⊙ ⊙) When Passing to Left of Overtaken Vessel.**

85 **Vessels in Overtaking Situations** including sailing vessels, that overtakes another is the *give-way* vessel and must keep clear of the vessel being overtaken. The overtaken vessel is the *stand-on* vessel and must maintain course and speed. You are in an overtaking situation if you are unable to see either the green or red sidelights of the other vessel—only its stern light will be visible. With the use of proper sound signals, pass on either side. The overtaking vessel sounds the signal which must be answered by the overtaken vessel.

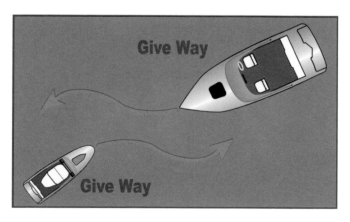

Figure 64. Powerboats Meeting Head-On

86 **Powerboats Meeting Head-On.** When two power-driven vessels meet bow to bow, neither is the stand-on vessel—both must take action. Each should sound one short blast and turn to starboard so as to pass port to port. With the use of proper signals, vessels may also pass starboard to starboard.

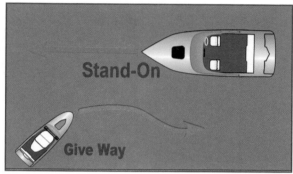

Figure 65. Powerboats Crossing

87 **Powerboats Crossing.** A power-driven vessel (including sailboats under power and PWCs) seeing another vessel crossing off its starboard side must keep clear (give-way). It is required to take early action to change course, slow down, or back down, until the other vessel passes. The other vessel is the stand-on vessel, but it is obligated to maintain course and speed until the give-way vessel clearly indicates its intentions. If the give-way vessel does not take timely action to avoid a collision, the stand-on vessel should take action to avoid a collision. The area on your starboard side from dead ahead to just aft of your starboard beam is your danger area. Assume that any boat in your danger area is the stand-on vessel and required to maintain course and speed.

88 **Right-of-Way.** This term applies to vessels on the Great Lakes and Western Rivers. A vessel downbound (with the current) has the right-of-way over upbound vessels, which are more maneuverable. The downbound vessel sounds a signal first and chooses the place of passing. Vessels crossing rivers must keep clear of vessels ascending or descending the river.

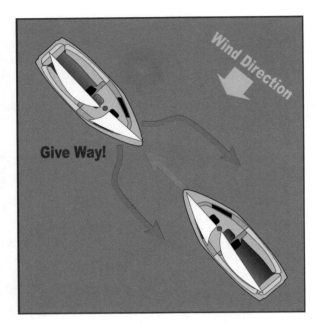

Wind Direction

Give Way!

Figure 66. Sailboats Approaching One Another

89 **Sailing Vessels Approaching One Another.** When two sailing vessels (not under power) approach one another, the position of the wind determines which vessel is the give-way vessel:

• If each vessel has the wind on a different side, the one with the wind on its port side keeps clear.

• If both have the wind on the same side, the vessel nearest to the direction of the wind keeps clear.

90 **Vessels in Restricted Visibility.** Except for the General Rule of Responsibility, entirely different rules apply when vessels are in restricted visibility:

• Proceed with utmost caution at a safe speed for the circumstances. A good rule is to proceed at a speed that will allow you to stop in half the distance of visibility. If all vessels follow this rule, the chance of collision is diminished.

• Display your running lights and sound the proper signals for your boat.

• Listen for signals from other vessels. Post a watch at both bow and stern. If necessary, stop your boat to listen, but keep the engine running so that you will be ready for immediate action.

• A special circumstance occurs when *more than two* vessels are involved in a meeting situation. Any options can be used to avoid collision. However, in restricted visibility, by convention, all vessels should turn to starboard. If this convention is observed, there is little risk of collision.

91 **Recognizing Vessels in Special Circumstances.** It is important to recognize by special signals or lights certain kinds of activity on other vessels. In Chapter 2, the requirements for navigation lights on recreational vessels were discussed. You should be able to recognize most such vessels by their lights. At the same time, you should presume that a vessel exhibiting any different pattern or color of navigation lights may be engaged in other activity and ought to be given wide passage.

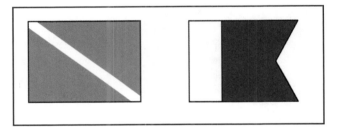

Figure 67. Red-and-White "Diver Below" Flag (Left) and International Code "A" Blue-and-White Flag (Right)

92 **Vessels Engaged in Diving** are restricted in their ability to maneuver when they have divers attached to the vessel. They are required to display the International Code "A" flag during daylight and at night to show three (3) vertical all-round lights, red-over-white-over-red.

93 If divers are free swimming, the vessel is *not* considered to be restricted in its ability to maneuver. The well-known *Diver Below* flag, (a red square with white diagonal

stripe) is distinctive from the International Code "A" flag described above. The *Diver Below* flag is usually flown from a boat, raft, float, or buoy to indicate the location of free swimming divers. Neither flag is exhibited when underway, or when divers are not in the water. Many states have local regulations governing diving and underwater operations. Boaters should stay well clear. Divers often stray from the diving vessel.

94 **Vessels Towing** can be identified by the lights displayed, two (2) forward white masthead lights arranged vertically and a yellow aft towing light above the sternlight. This applies when the combination of tug and its tow are no more than 650 feet long. When this length exceeds 650 feet, 3 forward white masthead lights are arranged vertically. A barge or other vessel being towed exhibits sidelights and a stern light. A vessel pushing ahead or towing alongside displays 2 white masthead lights in a vertical line and (in Inland Waters) 2 yellow towing lights aft in a vertical line with no stern light or (in International Waters) no yellow lights, just a stern light. A vessel being pushed displays a yellow flashing light on its bow as well as its sidelights.

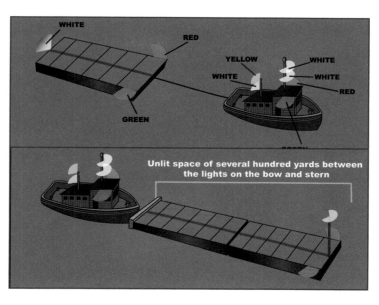

Figure 68. Tug Towing (Top), Tug Pushing (Bottom)

95 Accidents can occur at night with vessels towing or pushing because the barges are not always obvious. Tow lines are frequently long and always potentially hazardous. If you know the light patterns, you will be able to recognize a towing situation and stay well clear.

96 **Vessels Engaged in Fishing** or trawling are restricted in their ability to maneuver and display unique lights to indicate that. Fishing is using lines and nets (but not trolling) and vessels engaged in fishing show a red all-round light over a white all-round light. Trawling is dragging a net or scoop along the bottom, and a vessel so engaged shows a green light over a white one.

97 **Vessels Dredging or Engaged in Underwater Maneuvers** (in Inland Waters) display 3 all-round lights, red over white over red. You may also see 2 all-round red lights in a vertical line marking an obstruction or 2 all-round green lights showing the side where vessels may pass.

Adverse Conditions and Emergencies

98 Every boater would prefer to be on the water in pleasant weather and ideal conditions. Unfortunately, in spite of planning and preparation, you will at some point encounter bad weather, restricted visibility, and unpleasant situations such as running out of fuel, grounding, or needing to be towed. You may even find yourself involved with life-threatening situations such as people falling overboard, capsizing, swamping, collision, or serious medical emergencies. Seven out of ten boating fatalities occur on boats of 20 feet or less. Accidents occur on days with light winds, calm waters, and good visibility as well as in adverse conditions. Many accidents and injuries are preventable.

Life Preservers

99 One universal message for you to remember is—the importance of wearing a life preserver. They preserve lives. No sensible person goes aboard a boat without having the correct kind of life preserver available.

100 It is wise to put on a life preserver before you need it in rough seas or stormy weather. If passengers are not wearing life preservers, make sure they are available and accessible at all locations where passengers are likely to be. By the same token, if you're helping another vessel in some distress, it's always important to put your life jacket on before you get busy.

Running Out of Fuel

101 Running out of fuel can be inconvenient, sometimes dangerous, often expensive, and always embarrassing.

102 **Prevention.** Skippers should know their boat's maximum range with a full load of fuel. Until your own experience gives you more precise data, calculate your boat's range by using the information your manufacturer includes about the maximum rate of fuel consumption and usable fuel tank capacity. Remember that wind, current, or an engine problem may increase your fuel consumption. The gas gauge on your instrument panel is only a close approximation of the amount of fuel in the tank.

103 It is sensible to leave port with a full fuel tank and then not let it go below one-third full. It is useful to remember the 1/3 rule. That is, 1/3 of the tank to get there; 1/3 of the tank to get home; 1/3 of the tank for emergencies. This means not letting your tank get below one-third full. If followed, it also means never running out of fuel. Plan for extra fuel if you expect bad weather or strong currents.

104 **PWC Fuel.** Most PWCs have a small reserve tank of fuel onboard. Set the three position fuel selector switch on "Off" when you are not using your PWC, use the "On" position during normal operation, and the "Reserve" position if you run out of fuel in the "On" position. Head for home immediately if you need to use the "Reserve" setting; there is only a small amount of fuel available to you.

105 Every powered vessel has a particular cruising speed at which it operates most efficiently. The literature provided by the manufacturer should guide you well in determining this speed for your boat. In general, avoid running at full throttle. Fuel consumption increases dramatically at high speeds for most boats. Experiment with various throttle settings to find the most efficient speed for your boat. A fuel-flow meter can help.

106 Even if you are a trailer boater who normally stops for fuel at a gas station en route to or from the ramp, it is wise to know the location of fuel stations in the area where you cruise. Small-craft charts may list marine facilities. U.S. Coast Pilots and cruising guides will also have this information. If you carry extra fuel, carry it in approved tanks designed for use in a marine environment. Gasoline weighs 6.1 pounds per gallon, and this may add considerable weight to your boat. Always secure portable tanks so that they will not move around in the boat.

107 **Managing a Fuel Shortage.** You can get into trouble drifting with an empty fuel tank. Anchor if you are in a safe location. Check your chart and estimate your position. It is a good idea for everyone on board to be wearing a life preserver—with your boat disabled and unable to maneuver, there is no way to pick up a person in the water. Help may be available from a fellow boater. If you are off-shore or in a quiet cove, getting help may be more difficult.

108 If you have a VHF-FM radio onboard, you can contact the Coast Guard using Channel 16 if you are in an area they cover. You can ask them to contact a specific towing company or towing

network for you, or they can issue a general radio call to which any commercial tower in the area may respond. If you call the Coast Guard or a commercial company for help, be prepared to tell them where you are. The Coast Guard will not send one of their boats unless there is a life threatening emergency or a commercial service is not available in the area within a reasonable time. You can also call a towing company yourself on VHF-FM radio. Assistance may be available by contacting the local Marine Patrol by radio. Simply attracting the attention of another boater by signaling may be the solution for the small boat owner boating on a lake.

Grounding

109 Running aground (sometimes called *stranding*) is often more of a nuisance than a danger. Knowledge, fast work, and a little luck can often reduce the inconvenience to just a matter of minutes.

110 If you run aground, first check your hull. Rocks and stumps are hazards in many areas. Hitting an object at even moderate speed can crack or puncture a hull. With a hole in your hull, it is better to be aground than partially afloat and sinking, until you take corrective measures.

111 If you run aground on a rising tide, time will work with you. If it is a falling tide, you must work quickly, or you may be stranded for several hours.

112 A small boat with shallow draft is easier to free than a large, deep draft boat. Tilt outboard motors or stern drives into an up position to reduce draft at the transom. Do not run your engines; you may pump sand and mud into them.

113 With larger powerboats it may be possible to get afloat by shifting weight to the stern. Adults can sometimes push the boat into deeper water. Before attempting this, however, always make sure there is an easy way back into the boat. You may be able to float the boat off by rocking it from side to side to

create wave action. Small sailboats with their *centerboards* raised may also be freed in this manner. Be certain to wear life preservers and have safety lines attached when attempting any of these maneuvers.

114 Larger sailboats are more difficult to free when grounded. Several methods may be tried. Hoist a mainsail to a beam wind; the wind may help push you off. If aground with a larger sail or power boat, use a dinghy and firmly set an anchor some distance from the boat. Be sure you set the anchor into deepening water. The boat may come free by slowly hauling in the anchor rode.

Figure 69. Heeling a Sailboat to Reduce Draft

115 Heeling (leaning) a sailboat over to one side may reduce draft enough to free the keel from the ground. Move the crew to the low side. Place a heavy crew member at the end of the boom while holding it at right angles to the low side of the boat. If this does not work, try hoisting the mainsail to a beam wind; the wind may help push you off. Another way to heel the boat is to rig a halyard to an anchor set off the beam. Slowly winching in the halyard may sufficiently reduce the draft. You may ask another boater to pull on the halyard with his boat, but when pulling from the top of a mast be very care-

ful to avoid putting too much strain on the line. It could damage the rigging or jam the block at the masthead. You may also ask another boater to run past with his shallow draft boat thereby creating a wake that might lift you free.

Towing or Being Towed

116 You may be asked sometime to take another vessel in tow. It is a longstanding custom among boaters to offer assistance to each other. Taking another vessel in tow requires care and confidence in your own ability as a skipper. If there is imminent danger to persons or property and immediate action is necessary, act reasonably and responsibly. Do not place your own crew and vessel at undue risk. The Coast Guard or Marine Patrol does not need two vessels in distress. If you are not comfortable with providing a tow because of weather conditions or your own skill level, remember that you can also be of assistance by calling for help or by going yourself to get help for the vessel needing the tow.

117 **Towing Procedures.** Towing requires certain safety precautions with which you should be familiar:

- Everyone in both vessels should don life preservers.

- Tow lines must be strong. Nylon makes a good tow line because it stretches. Braided nylon is preferable to twisted nylon because twisted nylon has a greater "snap-back" action if it breaks. An anchor line from the boat being towed usually makes a good tow line.

- Never tie to an improperly mounted cleat. Cleats used for towing should always be through-bolted with a backing block to spread the strain. Don't use the cleat if you cannot see how it is mounted. Bow eye bolts and transom eye bolts, such as used to tow skiers, are usually adequately bolted.

- Keep passengers out of direct line with a tow rope in case it breaks or a deck fitting pulls out of the deck. A piece of hardware at the end of a stretched nylon tow line can be a lethal weapon.

- Fasten tow lines securely to both boats in a manner that does not interfere with steering. Steering will be difficult if you fasten a tow line to just one side of a boat. If you use cleats located on opposite sides of the transom, form a bridle by attaching a line securely between these eyes or cleats. Attach the tow line in the middle of the bridle.

- Keep outboard motors and stern-drives on the towed boat down and centered to prevent swinging to one side and then the other.

- If a small sailboat does not have a bow eye or bow cleat, tow it by fastening a tow line to the mast at the deck if the base of the mast is mounted on the keel. Keep the tow line centered by securing it to the headstay fitting. Raise the centerboard and secure the tiller or wheel. Make sure the sails are lowered.

- Adjust the length of the tow line so that the towed boat rides a minimum of three wave lengths behind the towing vessel. This ensures reasonable steering and prevents the towed boat from running up on the tow boat. Shorten a tow line when maneuvering in confined areas.

- Start moving slowly and tow slowly and steadily. Keep an eye on the tow line to be sure that it does not become tangled in the propeller of the towboat. See that the towed vessel rides properly in the water and does not overrun the towing boat.

- In the case of a smaller boat towing a larger one and when approaching a dock or moorage, it may be advantageous to tie up alongside the towed boat. If possible, keep the stern of the towed boat ahead of the rudder or lower unit of the towing boat. This method can reduce the effects of a crosswind and add greatly to maneuverability.

Man Overboard.

118 Falling overboard can be a very serious problem. With small boats it may not cause a critical problem. Small boats tend to be more maneuverable. A fall from a small boat is unlikely to cause injury. A small boat is also likely to be in sheltered waters during daylight hours with other boats around. The topsides are low so crawling back into the boat may not be difficult for young agile people. Falling overboard from a cruising boat in open water is a different matter. The victim may be older and less agile. It may be dark. The boat is much less maneuverable. There may be a sea running. There are no other boats around. You may not be missed immediately. Those left on board may have little experience, particularly with something like this. The topsides are high, so that recovery is difficult. Your water-soaked clothing is heavy, making it difficult to get back onboard. By far the best remedy is prevention. Take precautions not to fall overboard. **DON'T LET IT HAPPEN TO YOU.**

119 **Prevention.** There are some things you can do to lessen the chances of falling overboard. Passengers should not stand in small boats underway or sit with their legs dangling over the side. Deck-gripping shoes are the best footwear; bare feet are not acceptable. Keep your weight low and close to the centerline when moving around in small boats. Equip sailboats with through-bolted life-line stanchions and install safety netting if there are children aboard. In bad weather, attach crew members to special safety lines with harnesses. It is difficult to find and recover a person lost overboard, especially in poor visibility.

120 **Recovery Procedures.** Shout *"Man Overboard"* immediately to everyone on board and especially to your helmsman. If the victim is not wearing a life preserver, toss one to him, even if he can swim. It will mark the site and give the victim something buoyant to grasp. Assign someone to point constantly at the victim and never let the victim

out of sight. Reduce speed and begin to turn the boat as quickly as possible so that the boat stays close as possible to the victim.

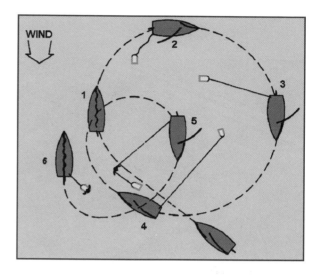

Figure 70. Man Overboard Recovery

121 Under sail, use the Quick-Stop maneuver. Sailing with main and jib only, immediately head up and tack
1. Leave the jib cleated to slow the boat.
2. If a Lifesling system is hung on the stern pulpit with the polypropylene line attached to the boat, remove the Lifesling from its bag and throw it overboard.
3. If upwind of the victim, continue the turn to fall off the wind. The jib will be aback and hasten the turn. The jib may now be roller furled or dropped on deck inside the lifelines still cleated.
4. Straighten out until abeam of the victim, heading directly downwind; then jibe.
5. Continue the turnaround to a position just a boat length to leeward of the victim.
6. Continue to circle the victim to draw the trailing line in toward the victim until contact is made. The victim dons the Lifesling and the boat turns into the wind with the victim on the windward side. Stop the engine and drop the sails. Pull the victim in, head-high and secure the line.

122 It is extremely difficult to get a man overboard out of the water and back aboard. This is true even with strong swimmers in life jackets and in excellent physical condition. In a real life-threatening crisis, the difficulty is increased because people are tired, cold, exhausted, and frightened.

Figure 71. Low Freeboard Recovery

124 In a boat with low freeboard, you may be able to assist a person to climb aboard. To prevent capsizing a small boat you may need to move weight to the opposite side. The best location to bring a person aboard in a small boat—if the water is calm enough—is over the transom. Be alert to the presence of hot outboard motors, sharp propellers, or depth sounder brackets.

125 On larger boats with a full crew, lift the victim aboard. Shorthanded, use a swim platform, ladder, or winch the victim aboard. Ladders generally work well only in calm conditions and when the person in the water is still in good shape. Their use by anyone weakened by cold or the exertion of swimming has proven ineffective and can be dangerous in rough water, especially those mounted on the transom. In rough water bring the victim to the boat amidships. Improvised hoisting slings using nets or sails to scoop up the victim have proven very difficult to use. Other improvised solutions such as a rope ladder, or a knotted line may not work effectively under adverse conditions. Have proper recovery equipment aboard before going out.

126 To winch someone aboard, connect a block and tackle (the boom vang tackle on a sailboat, for example) to the main halyard shackle and raise the main halyard until the shackle end is some ten feet above the deck. Secure the halyard. On a powerboat connect to a high secure point such as a padeye on the fly bridge. Connect the other end of the block and tackle to the Lifesling harness. Reeve the bitter end of the block and harness line through a turning block near the windward rail (the jib sheet block, for example) and then to a winch. Winch the victim up and over the life lines. On a power boat without a winch, use hoisting tackle with 5:1 purchase.

127 These procedures assume the victim is conscious and rational, and that he has been able to grab the sling or line. If the victim is unconscious or weak, a strong swimmer can go overboard with the sling and a life jacket on or a safety line and life jacket on and be retrieved with the victim. Remember if you send someone into the water to help, there are now two people to get back aboard instead of one.

128 Practice whatever procedure you plan to use before an incident occurs. When recovering someone under adverse conditions is not the best time to be learning or practicing the procedure.

Restricted Visibility

129 Rain, fog, smog, hail, or snow may restrict visibility. Your primary concern in restricted visibility is to avoid collision. See and be seen; hear and be heard. Make every effort to detect other boats and to make your presence known to them. When operating in restricted visibility, the following procedures are recommended:

- Reduce speed—Navigation Rules require it. You should be able to stop your boat in one-half the distance you can see. If another vessel looms up ahead of you and it is following the same precaution, collision will be unlikely.

- Put on life preservers as a precautionary measure.

- If available, post lookouts—persons whose only task will be looking and listening.

- Turn on your navigation lights.

- Sound the proper sound signals for your vessel. Powerboats sound 1 prolonged (4 to 6 sec) blast every 2 minutes. Sailing vessels (no power) sound 1 prolonged blast followed by 2 short blasts every 2 minutes.

- Briefly shut down your engine, if absolutely necessary, to listen for sounds of nearby boats and navigational aids. If you hear a signal, reply with your own signal, and proceed cautiously until you determine their position. The direction of sound is difficult to determine in a fog.

- Determine your position as accurately as possible and plot the safest course to your destination. Try to run from one lighted navigational aid to another. Avoid a course that brings you close to hazards. Never take undue risks to get home.

- If lost, anchor and wait for conditions to improve. You will save fuel and avoid becoming further disoriented.

Swamping and Capsizing

130 Swamping occurs when your boat fills with water. Capsizing occurs when your boat overturns. Capsizing and falling overboard account for the majority of boating fatalities. *Always stay with the boat if you swamp or capsize.*

Figure 72. Swamped or Capsized Boat

131 A boat is easier to see than a person in the water—and as such—is itself a distress signal easily seen by passing vessels. Few people have the strength and endurance to swim more than a short distance, especially if the water is cold. Shore is always farther away than it appears. A person can hang on to a floating boat or object much longer than he will be able to swim. And the person will be able to keep more of his body out of the water, retaining body heat. Everyone now in the water should be wearing a life preserver. If not, and the preservers are still accessible, put them on now.

132 Stay calm—Encourage others to do the same. You may be able to turn the boat right side up, bail it, and paddle towards shore, even using hands for paddles.

Collision

133 Collision is the most frequent type of boating accident. Most boating collisions happen to experienced operators in daylight, around midday, on weekends when visibility is excellent and weather is good.

134 Collisions occur because of high speed, lack of a lookout, and operators simply not looking where they are going. Today's high-speed boats and personal watercraft cover a significant distance in a short time. The distraction of the operator for just a few moments can cause a collision.

135 If involved in a collision, the actions you take depend on the severity of the accident. Your first order of business is to account for and check the condition of your crew and then the passengers and the occupants of the other boat. Immediately apply first aid if there is any serious injury. Don't be in a hurry to pull the boats apart. Two boats jammed together but still floating are better than two damaged boats sinking.

136 Seriously injured persons must be given expert medical attention as soon as possible. Call to nearby boats for help, and to the Coast Guard by radio. You must know your location whenever placing a distress call.

137 Instruct all passengers to put on life preservers. Then determine the degree of damage to the vessels. Will they stay afloat? Check for hull damage and make necessary emergency repairs.

138 An operator observing any kind of boating accident must stop, and render assistance to those in danger, providing he does not place his vessel or passengers at risk.

139 Federal law protects from liability a person who in good faith renders assistance at the scene of an accident without objection of the person being assisted.

Fire

140 On shore a person can run away from a fire and call the fire department. On a boat, there is nowhere to go except into the water, and help may be far away.

141 **Fire Prevention.** Most fires are preventable. Correct any condition that may contribute to a fire.
- Inspect your bilges frequently. Most fires result from starting engines with gasoline vapors in the bilge. This type of fire spreads rapidly. Diesel fuel will burn as fast as gasoline when ignited. The only difference is that the temperature at which its vapor will ignite is higher.
- When fueling, ground the fuel line nozzle against the fill pipe to eliminate static sparks that could ignite fuel vapors. Ventilate the engine compartment after every fueling until you are sure there are no dangerous vapors. Sniff for vapors and check for leaks.
- Keep your bilge free of grease, oil, and debris. Regularly inspect electrical wiring. Repair any bare wires or loose electrical connections immediately to prevent a spark from igniting fuel vapors. Use marine parts for repairs.
- Store dinghy fuel and propane so it has plenty of ventilation, preferably topside. Be careful if you carry charcoal on your boat; if allowed to get damp, it can ignite from spontaneous combustion.

142 **Responding to Fire.** (See Fire Extinguishers in Chapter 2.) Follow these steps if fire breaks out while underway:
- Immediately notify everyone aboard. Tell them the location of the fire. Be sure they are wearing life jackets. Instruct them to move to the unaffected portion of the boat, usually toward the wind.
- If the fire is aft, try to keep it downwind by heading the boat into the wind. If it is near the bow, put the stern into the wind.

Figure 73. Keep Fire Downwind

- Turn off all fuel supplies—engine, galley stove, heaters. Disconnect all sources of electrical power.
- Identify the source of the fire.
- Choose the correct extinguisher. You can make a fire worse by using the wrong type of extinguisher.Use water on an alcohol stove fire. Water will mix with alcohol and dilute it to the point where it cannot burn. Never use water on a class B flammable liquid fire. Oil and gasoline will float on the water and spread the fire. Use your dry chemical extinguishers for all fires other than alcohol.
- Remember **PASS**:

  Pull the safety pin.

  Aim at the base of the fire.

  Squeeze the handle or lever.

  Sweep from side to side.

- Make sure there is a clear exit behind you and hold the unit upright. Aim the nozzle at the base of the fire from 6 to 8 feet away and sweep from side to side or use a series of short blasts aimed at the base. Too much pressure from the extinguisher can cause liquids or grease to spatter and spread the fire.
- Watch for hot embers and repeat if flashback occurs.
- If unable to get the fire under control at once, call *MayDay* on VHF Channel 16. You can always advise the Coast Guard later if it is no longer a MAYDAY situation. Be prepared to tell the Coast Guard where you are located.

- Display a visual distress signal to attract local boats. It is advantageous to have someone standing by to help.
- If there is the slightest doubt about whether you can put out the fire, don't even try. Immediately get the people off your boat and as far away from the fire as possible.
- On a PWC, stop the engine immediately. Take your distress signals and swim as far away from the craft as you can. Keep all occupants together until help arrives. Shore is probably farther away that it appears to be. Do not try to reach the shore unless you are certain before starting that you can swim that far.
- Know how to use an extinguisher in advance—do not try to read the label when a fire is in progress. Local fire departments provide practice opportunities, or you may be able to arrange one.

Medical Emergencies on the Water

143 You are often isolated from immediate medical help when an accident or injury occurs on the water. You must be self-sufficient. Be prepared by taking medical treatment courses such as life-saving, first-aid, and cardiopulmonary resuscitation (CPR) courses offered by organizations such as the American Red Cross. This is particularly important if you are a boater who regularly sails out of range of immediate medical help or takes extended long distance cruises. Keep a manual and well-equipped first-aid kit on board. (See the Red Cross recommendations for a first-aid kit, that follows.)

144 *Certain information on medical emergencies in this chapter has been extracted from the 1994 edition of* First Aid Fast, *a publication of the American Red Cross. The United States Power Squadrons is grateful to the American Red Cross for their permission to use this information in this student manual.*

145 First Aid Fast *is an integral part of Red Cross training, but by itself it does not constitute complete and comprehensive training. The book is designed to familiarize persons with emergencies that can happen and to prepare them to react before an emergency occurs. It also provides a quick source for information in emergencies, guiding a person's actions in a step-by-step manner. The booklet is available from local chapters of the American Red Cross.*

146 **First Aid Kit.** *From* First Aid Fast *by The American Red Cross.* Be prepared for an emergency. Keep a first-aid kit in your home, in your automobile, and on your boat. Carry a first aid kit with you, or know where you can find one when you are participating in outdoor activities. Know the location of first-aid kits where you work. A first-aid kit should include the following:
- Flashlight and batteries
- Scissors and tweezers
- Emergency blanket
- Triangular bandages
- Antiseptic towelettes
- Band-Aids in assorted sizes
- Gauze pads
- Roller gauze
- Adhesive tape
- Antiseptic ointment
- Disposable gloves
- Plastic bags
- Cold pack
- Activated charcoal

147 **Attacks, Cardiac Arrest, and Drowning.** The most important factor in saving a person needing emergency respiration is getting air into the lungs quickly. Ideally, someone on board has training in rescue breathing and cardiopulmonary resuscitation (CPR). Give rescue breathing to a person who is unconscious and not breathing. Give CPR to a person who is not breathing and does not have a pulse.

149 Don't wait for an emergency to be convinced of the need for rescue breathing and CPR training. Organizations such as The American Red Cross offer these courses. Sign up for a course as soon as possible.

150 **Hypothermia** is the abnormal lowering of the body's internal temperature due to loss of heat from exposure to cold air, wind, or water. It can occur even on a bright, sunny day. It is life-threatening cold, but not the type of cold you feel on a cold day. The effects of hypothermia appear more quickly in water than in air and much more quickly in cold water. Be particularly careful in northern lakes in late spring when the water temperatures are still very low. More victims of marine accidents lose their lives from hypothermia than from drowning. The use of alcohol accelerates the onset of hypothermia.

151 To delay the occurrence of hypothermia, dress warmly, and stay dry and out of the wind. If you fall into the water, and are wearing a life jacket, you can delay hypothermia by remaining inactive. A life jacket lessens the need to move around in the water, and will help retain body heat.

Figure 74.
HELP Position

152 Alone in the water, hold the inner side of your arms tightly against the side of your chest; press your thighs together and raise them, to close off the groin region where blood vessels are close to the surface. This is the HELP position (Heat Escape Lessening Posture) as seen in Figure 74.

Figure 75. HUDDLE Position

153 When there is more than one person in the water, the HUDDLE position seen in Figure 75 is recommended. Victims huddle together as a group with chests side by side and arms around each other's shoulders to share body warmth.

154 Hypothermia is a particular threat to PWC operators because of the constant exposure to wind and water. If you become fatigued or start to feel cold, pay attention to your body's warning signs and head for home.

155 **Red Cross Health and Safety Programs.** The Red Cross offers a variety of community programs that teach life saving skills and safety information. Contact your local Red Cross chapter for information on these and other programs:

American Red Cross Adult CPR*
American Red Cross Basic Aid Training (for children)*
American Red Cross Community CPR*
American Red Cross Infant & Child CPR*
American Red Cross Standard First Aid*
American Red Cross `Till Help Arrives*
American Red Cross Community Water Safety
American Red Cross Learn to Swim Programs
American Red Cross Longfellow's Whale Tales (for children)
*Available in Spanish

156 **Carbon Monoxide Poisoning.** Carbon monoxide poisoning is the cause of a startling number of boating fatalities. Often called the "silent killer," carbon monoxide is a colorless, odorless, and tasteless gas. It is the result of incomplete burning of any material containing carbon, such as gasoline, diesel oil, alcohol, natural gas, propane, or charcoal. Boat engines, cabin heaters, generators, and galley stoves produce carbon monoxide.

157 Extremely toxic even in small quantities, carbon monoxide can combine with the blood 250 times as readily as oxygen and will accumulate in the blood over a long period of time. It is often impossible to detect carbon monoxide before it overcomes a victim, who is then too weak to escape or summon help. Although carbon monoxide in

---

HYPOTHERMIA
From *First Aid Fast* by The American Red Cross
SIGNALS
• Shivering, numbness, glassy stare
• Apathy, weakness, impaired judgment
• Loss of consciousness
CARE
• CHECK the scene and the person.
• Send someone to call for an ambulance. [On the water, radio for medical assistance on Ch 16.]
• Gently move the person to a warm place.
• CHECK breathing and pulse.
• Give rescue breathing and CPR as necessary.
• Remove any wet clothing and dry the person.
• Warm the person SLOWLY by wrapping in blankets or by putting dry clothing on the person. Hot water bottles and chemical hot packs may be used when first wrapped in a towel or blanket before applying.
• DO NOT WARM THE PERSON TOO QUICKLY, such as immersing him or her in warm water. Rapid warming can cause dangerous heart rhythms.

itself has no telltale odor, it may mix with other gases that do have an odor. The odor of exhaust fumes almost guarantees the presence of carbon monoxide. However, carbon monoxide may accumulate in areas exclusive of exhaust fumes. The most prevalent source of carbon monoxide is exhaust from engines and generators. Breaks, cracks, or leaks in exhaust systems are the most frequent conditions leading to fatalities, according to the American Boat and Yacht Council. Related to this is the exhaust from a boat's engines. The forward motion of the boat creates a back draft at the stern that pulls the exhaust into the cockpit or cabin. When you detect this exhaust, open windshields and portholes to create a draft through the boat so that fumes will exit.

158 Prevent carbon monoxide buildup by regularly checking your engine and generator exhaust systems and the seals around your hatches and portholes for leaks. Check the ventilation of your alcohol stove. Maintain your generators meticulously. Carbon monoxide can leak from them without your knowing it. It is a good idea to run your exhaust blowers while using them. You may not want to run them while you are sleeping.

159 Dangerous effects of carbon monoxide can occur when a boat is at a marina dock, anchored, or rafted up with other boats. With engines idling or generators running to provide electricity, carbon monoxide can easily drift into your boat from nearby vessels, especially if your hatches or portholes are open. Carbon monoxide detectors are available that feature not only a visual alert but an audible alarm. The latter is most desirable for it will sound when carbon monoxide concentration in your boat becomes dangerous. Consider one of these detectors as a vital part of your safety equipment.

160 The symptoms of mild carbon monoxide poisoning are nearly the same as seasickness, colds, flu, nausea, weakness, dizziness, headache, ringing-in-the-ears, and watering of eyes. Severe poisoning can result in brain or heart damage or death. A sign of severe poisoning is often a cherry-red coloring to the skin.

161 If you suspect carbon monoxide poisoning, get medical help at once. Treatment consists of immediately getting the victim to breathe large quantities of fresh air. Give supplementary oxygen if available. If breathing has stopped, start rescue breathing immediately. Watch for a relapse. Victims often respond quickly but collapse later because vital organs are damaged from lack of oxygen.

Marine Radiotelephone

162 The best radiotelephone system for recreational boats is the VHF radio. VHF means Very High Frequency, the part of the radio spectrum in which it operates. VHF radios have a range of only 20 to 30 miles, but they usually provide clear, static-free messages. Vessels cruising beyond this range will need long-range SSB (single side-band) radiotelephone equipment.

Licensing Requirements

163 You do *not* need a license to operate a VHF radio, radar, or EPIRB (Emergency Position Indicating Radio Beacon) on your recreational boat of less than 20 meters (65.6 feet) in U.S. waters.

164 You *do* need a ship's station license issued by the Federal Communications Commission if you:

• Operate a boat over 65 feet (20 meters) in length
• Travel to foreign ports or talk to foreign stations
• Use a SSB radio or Inmarsat equipment

165 A restricted radiotelephone operator's permit may be necessary to visit a foreign country. For information about licenses and fees, contact the FCC Customer Assistance Hotline (1-888-225-5322)(www.fcc.gov).

Operating Procedures

166 You may legally use your VHF radio only for distress, safety, operational, and public correspondence communications. Distress and safety communications include calls relating to danger to life and property, safety bulletins, weather warnings, and talking with other boats to avoid collision. Operational communications include calls relating to navigational information, and to arrange for supplies, accommodations, repairs, and meeting other vessels. Public correspondence communications include calls made through a marine radiotelephone operator that connect a boat radio to the shore public telephone network. Note: The increased popularity and usage of cellular telephones have made public correspondence channels uneconomical and they are being phased out for other uses. VHF remains the preferred means of calling the USCG.

Choose the Correct Channel

167 Recreational boaters may legally use only a few of the many channels available. The channels designated for recreational boating use are listed in Table XI. (Data from FCC as of 21 AUG 2001.)

168 **Listen to Channel 16.** The rules require that if you are underway with your radio turned on, it must be tuned to Channel 16, the distress, safety, and calling channel. Channel 09 is also a calling channel for recreational boats in most areas. Check with local law enforcement agencies to learn the procedure for your area.

169 Your safety and that of fellow boaters depends on someone hearing a call for assistance. Your listening on this channel makes sure that a large number of boats will hear an emergency call.

TABLE XI • MARINE VHF RADIOTELEPHONE CHANNEL USAGE		
Communication Purpose	**Channel Number**	**Description**
Distress, Safety, & Calling	16	A required channel on all VHF radios. For ship-to-ship and ship-to-coast communications. Used for distress calls and for initial contact with other vessels or shore stations. Ch 16 is monitored by the U.S. Coast Guard as well as harbor masters, marinas, fuel docks, and other shore stations. After contact on Ch 16, you must switch to a working channel.
Coast Guard Liaison & Marine Safety Information	22A	Used for contact with Coast Guard ship, coast, and aircraft stations after first establishing communications on Ch 16.
Ship to Coast, & Ship to Ship "Calling Channel"	09	For communications with marinas and public docks and for contacting commercial vessels about matters of common concern. In some areas Channel 09 is also an alternate calling channel for non-commercial vessels, supplementing Channel 16.
Ship to Ship & Ship to Coast "Working Channels"	68,69,71, 72,78	For use after initial contact on a calling channel. Channel 72 is a ship-to-ship working channel only. (In the Great Lakes area, channels 79 and 80 are also used as working channels by recreational boats, sharing these with commercial traffic. In Puget Sound and the Straits of Juan de Fuca, recreational vessels may also use Channel 67 as a working channel, sharing this channel with commercial vessels.)
Intership Safety	6	Required on all VHF radios. Used only for safety-oriented communications such as the avoidance of collision, and for search and rescue.
Port Operations	12, 14, 20, 66, 73, 74	For use by facilities directing the movement of vessels in or near ports, locks, and waterways.
Bridge to Bridge Navigation Safety	13	For contacting other vessels about meeting and passing situations and talking with locks and bridges. Low power operation (1 Watt) is required except in an emergency.
Distress, Safety, & General Purpose	70	For boats equipped with Digital Selective Calling equipment. Voice communications are not allowed. (When fully implemented, all VHF radios will be DSC compatible. A DSC transceiver can send information to other DSC receivers with the sender's ID, position, nature of distress, and contact channel.)

170 **Special Words.** The use of special procedural words helps to make messages clearer and shorter. However, both the sender and listener must learn to use them properly.
Affirmative: You are correct.
Negative: No.
Out: I am through talking and I do not expect you to reply.
Over: I am through talking and expect you to reply.
Roger: I understood your last call OK.

171 Police departments and CB radio sometimes use "ten" Codes. These are *not* used on marine VHF radio.

Emergency Calls

172 There are three emergency signals that have priority on any VHF channel—especially Channel 16—Distress, Urgency, and Safety.

173 **Distress Signal—MAYDAY.** This is a call to ask for assistance if there is immediate danger to life or property. A MAYDAY call has priority over all other radio calls. Use a MAYDAY call only for life-threatening medical emergencies or if your boat is sinking or on fire. A MAYDAY situation can be hectic. A readily available, partially-completed Distress Communication Form will be of great help in making an organized distress call. You will find a sample of this form at the end of this chapter.

174 You will need the following information if you make a MAYDAY call:
• An accurate location of your boat.
• A good description of your boat.
• The number of people on board.
• A description of the problem.

175 **Urgency Signal—PAN-PAN.**
(Pronounced *pahn-pahn.*) Use this signal when there is a threat to the safety of a person or boat, but the threat is not as serious as in a MAYDAY call. Examples of PAN-PAN calls are: loss of a person overboard, running out of fuel, losing your way in a fog, getting entangled in fishing gear, or being unable to control or operate your vessel. A prepared Distress Communication Form will also help you with this type of call.

176 **Safety Signal—SECURITY.**
(Pronounced *say-cure-it-tay.*) Use this signal for navigation safety messages. You will hear it used before weather alerts, warnings of navigational hazards, and operational signals (such as when a boat is backing out of a slip or approaching a blind bend). You may use this call to report a hazard such as a partially-sunken object in a busy channel.

177 **Responding to an Emergency Call.**
Unless you are in a position to help, do not use your radio on a channel being used for an emergency until you hear a *Silence Fini* (All Clear) announcement. If you are in a position to assist and are sure you are not interfering with other distress-related calls, call the vessel in distress and tell them what help you can offer. Meanwhile, make every effort to contact the Coast Guard.

Routine Calls

178 A VHF radio has a low/high power switch to increase power from 1 watt to 25 watts for longer range transmissions. Low power (1 watt) is enough for many communications. If you use low power you will be less apt to interfere with the calls of other vessels. To make a _ call to another boat:

• Listen on the calling channel (Channel 16 or 09) for at least 30 seconds to be sure you will not interfere with a conversation already in progress. Make sure that the squelch control on your radio is set just at the point where it cancels out static, but not so far up that it prevents your hearing other radio traffic. If you do not do this, you can destroy the value of two calls: your own and the message of another boat.

• If the channel is clear, push down the talk button on your microphone. Hold the microphone one inch from your mouth, and slowly call the name of the other boat in a normal tone of voice:

"ANNIE—THIS IS—QUEEN"

- Always start a broadcast with the name of the boat you are calling and the name of your boat. Repeat the name of the boat you are calling, 2 or 3 times if necessary. This first call should not exceed 30 seconds. If you do not make contact, wait at least 2 minutes before repeating the call. Repeat this procedure no more than three times. If you do not make contact during this period, wait 15 minutes before making your next try.

"QUEEN, THIS IS ANNIE. REPLY 68."

- ANNIE has responded with instructions to switch to Channel 68 (a working channel). QUEEN responds:

"68" or *"ROGER."*

- "Roger" means "I received your last call OK." Both vessels then switch to Channel 68.

QUEEN on 68: *"ANNIE."*

ANNIE on 68: *"QUEEN."*

- Continue with your message. Think before you speak and make your message simple. It must be about your boat's business and no longer than 3 minutes in length. Chit chat is not permitted.

- Each boat then acknowledges completion of the call, and returns to the calling frequency:

"QUEEN—OUT."

"ANNIE—OUT."

NOAA Weather Channels

179 Channels WX–1 through WX–10 offer around-the-clock broadcasts of latest weather information. Taped weather messages are repeated every 4 to 6 minutes and updated several times a day (more often when unusual weather develops). The Canadian Weather Department uses WX-4.

Hand-Held VHF Radios

180 Boaters often use hand-held VHF radios on small craft such as runabouts and daysailers. It is illegal for a recreational boater to use any marine VHF radio on shore. This includes hand-held radios and radios installed in trailerable boats. Use marine radiotelephones only on the water.

Prohibited Communications

181 Boat owners are responsible for the use of their marine radiotelephones. Improper use can result in substantial penalties.

- It is a criminal offense to use profane or indecent words, language, or meaning on a radio.

- Children should not be allowed to use a marine radio (it is not a plaything).

- Making a false MAYDAY or any phony call to the Coast Guard is a felony. These calls cost time and money and have tied up emergency channels resulting in the loss of life. Special equipment is now being used to put an end to these abuses.

EPIRB
Emergency Position
Indicating Radio Beacon

182 There are two types of EPIRB systems in use on recreational boats at present. Older units transmit an analog signal on 121.5 MHz. Newer units transmit a digital identification code on 406 MHz plus a low power homing signal on 121.5 MHz. Once activated (automatically or manually) the 406 MHz signal is instantly detected by geo-stationary satellites covering most of Earth. The 406 MHz EPIRBs incorporate a Global Positioning System (GPS) receiver to pinpoint position. The alert is transmitted to Mission Control Centers which alert Search and Rescue resources nearest to the EPIRB. The older EPIRBs lacking the GPS feature require that low-orbit satellites receive and localize the general location of the EPIRB signal. This old system is slow and requires up to two hours to process. The intent is to phase out the older system. Looming on the horizon is the Inmarsat E 1646 MHz (1.6 GHz) float-free, automatically-activated EPIRB which is detectable by Inmarsat geostationary satellites. The new system is recognized by

GMDSS, but is not currently available in the U.S. The FCC is studying recognition of these superior devices. **Note:** All 406 MHz EPIRBSs must be registered with NOAA and the 1.6 GHz units must be registered with Inmarsat prior to being deployed for potential emergency use.

Cellular Telephones

181 Cellular telephones have literally replaced public correspondence VHF channels which are being phased out. However, they cannot substitute for VHF marine radiotelephones in emergencies because of these serious limitations:

- Cellular telephones do not produce a general broadcast that can be heard by other boaters who might be able to render assistance.

- Cellular telephones do not provide direct contact with Coast Guard vessels or aircraft. This severely limits the ability to communicate directly with rescue craft. This lack of contact with potential rescuers eliminates communication that could be life-saving in severe emergencies.

- Cellular telephones do not provide a signal which the Coast Guard radio direction finding equipment can home-in on to determine a vessel's position.

- Cellular telephones broadcast at 3 watts while VHF marine radios broadcast at 25 watts. This further diminishes cellular telephones' usefulness in emergencies because of range.

Distress Communications Form

Complete this form now (except for items 6 through 9) and post it near your radiotelephone

Speak: SLOWLY—CLEARLY—CALMLY

1. Make sure the radiotelephone is turned "On."
2. Select either *VHF Channel 16 (156.8 MHz) or 2182 kHz.*
3. Press the microphone button, hold it close to your lips without touching them and say:
   "MAYDAY—MAYDAY—MAYDAY"
4. Say:
   "THIS IS _____, _____, _____."
                    your boat's name   your boat's name   your boat's name
5. Say:
   "MAYDAY, _____
                    your boat's name
6. Tell where you are. (What navigational aids or landmarks are near?)
7. State the nature of your emergency.
8. Give the number of adults and children aboard and the condition of any who may be injured.
9. Estimate the present seaworthiness of the boat.
10. Briefly describe the boat.
    "_____" State Registration Number.
    "_____" Length of the boat. "_____" Draft of the boat
    "_____" Type of boat. "_____" Hull color. "_____" Trim color
    "_____" Masts. "_____" Power. "_____" Construction
    Say anything else you think will help someone find you.
11. Say:
    "I WILL BE LISTENING ON CHANNEL 16 (2182)."
12. Say:
    "THIS IS _____**, OVER."**
                     your boat's name
13. Now, release the microphone button and listen.

    Make sure the volume control is about halfway to maximum and the "Squelch" control is all the way to minimum.

    Someone should answer immediately. If not, go back to step 3 and repeat the call.

    If there is still no answer and you hear a "hissing" sound when you release the microphone button, make sure the "Power" or "Level" or "H/L" control is in the high power "H" or "25 Watt" position. There may also be a "CH16" button to push.

    Do not panic. Stay calm and make sure the radiotelephone is working. When you press the microphone button a red (green) light should illuminate on the controls.

Rules to Live By • Review

Name .... Date .... Group No. ....

1. An aid to navigation is any object external to the boat that:
   1) helps a boater pilot a boat safely,
   2) aids a boater in finding position and
   3) _____
   a. marks the best fishing holes.
   b. provides a place to tie to.
   c. warns a boater of danger.
   d. marks an area with water depths of at least 50 feet.

2. Navigational marks can be identified at night by their _____ and sound characteristics.
   a. height
   b. shape
   c. width
   d. light

3. When returning from sea in U.S. waters, solid red starboard side-of-channel marks will have:
   a. no numbers or letters.
   b. odd numbers decreasing in value.
   c. letters only appearing in alphabetical order.
   d. even numbers increasing in value.

4. In the U.S. system, lighted navigation marks showing the port side of a channel when returning from sea have:
   a. green lights.
   b. yellow lights.
   c. red lights.
   d. white lights.

5. You are returning from sea and want to stay safely in the preferred channel. On what side of your boat would you keep a red and green horizontally-banded mark if the top band is red?
   a. either side would be appropriate.
   b. port
   c. you would stop and turn around (you are in an exclusion area).
   d. starboard

6. In the Uniform State Waterway Marking System, regulatory marks with orange circles and black lettering indicate:
   a. controlled areas.
   b. dangerous areas.
   c. exclusion areas where boats should keep out.
   d. general information for the area.

7. According to the Navigation Rules, who is responsible for complying with the rules?
   a. only the boat owner.
   b. only the operators of power boats.
   c. the owner, master, and crew.
   d. the boat's navigator.

8. The General Rule of Responsibility:
   a. is only applicable in International Waters.
   b. provides that you may break the Navigation Rules to avoid immediate danger.
   c. prescribes the insurance you must carry on your boat.
   d. describes who is responsible for equipping vessels with proper lights.

9. **A sailing vessel with sails raised, engine running, and propeller engaged is a:**
   a. vessel not under command.
   b. vessel restricted in her ability to maneuver.
   c. fast vessel.
   d. power-driven vessel.

10. **The vessel that according to the Navigation Rules must stay out of another vessel's way and take early and substantial action to do so by altering course and/or speed is called the _____ vessel.**
    a. stand-on
    b. in-danger
    c. give-way
    d. high priority

11. **You are fishing for bluefish by trolling a lure behind your slow-moving boat. According to the rules you have:**
    a. special privileges, providing you show the lights of a vessel engaged in fishing.
    b. priority of movement over all other vessels.
    c. no special rights or privileges.
    d. special privileges, for you are restricted in maneuverability.

12. **The "doubt" or "danger" signal used to express disagreement with an intended maneuver is:**
    a. 1 short blast of the whistle.
    b. 5 or more short and rapid blasts of the whistle.
    c. shouting *danger* as loudly as possible.
    d. rapid and constant waving of the arms.

13. **While operating in a thick fog, you hear 1 prolonged blast every 2 minutes. You proceed slowly and watch for a_____**
    a. vessel not under command.
    b. vessel engaged in fishing.
    c. sailing vessel underway.
    d. powerboat underway.

14. **You are required to proceed at a safe speed and maintain a lookout at all times when underway. A proper lookout is a major factor in:**
    a. finding lines of demarcation.
    b. measuring water temperature to determine the calmest waters.
    c. determining the accuracy of the compass heading.
    d. preventing collisions.

15. **When operating in a narrow channel, you must keep your vessel:**
    a. as close to the center of the channel as is safe and practicable.
    b. as close to the outer limit of the channel that lies to your port side as is safe and practicable.
    c. as close to the outer limit of the channel that lies to your starboard side as is safe and practicable.
    d. with the wind and current on your stern for best control.

16. **When two powerboats meet bow-to-bow, which boat must stay out of the way of the other?**
    a. the boat closest to the wind.
    b. both boats are give-way vessels.
    c. the boat closest to a northerly heading.
    d. the boat last to sound its maneuvering signal.

17. **A powerboat observing another vessel crossing its course from off its starboard side must:**
    a. speed up to pass ahead of the other vessel.
    b. maintain course and speed.
    c. take early action to keep clear.
    d. signal five short blasts on its whistle.

18. **If you see a red square-shaped flag with a white diagonal stripe you will know that it indicates the location of:**
    a. a sunken fishing reef.
    b. free-swimming divers.
    c. a spoils dumping ground.
    d. a water ski area.

19. **If you see two white lights in a vertical line, you should be prepared to take action because you are meeting a:**
    a. surfaced submarine.
    b. large sport fisherman.
    c. vessel towing or pushing ahead.
    d. night-time sail race.

20. **To avoid running out of fuel, determine the usable capacity of your fuel tank and your boat's rate of fuel consumption, and then:**
    a. bring extra fuel in easy-to-pour containers such as plastic milk jugs.
    b. plan to use 1/3 of the tank to reach your destination, 1/3 to get home, and 1/3 for emergencies.
    c. plan on enough fuel to get to the next fuel dock.
    d. plan on 1/2 of the tank to reach your destination and 1/2 of the tank to get home.

21. **If you run aground, your first action should be to:**
    a. put your boat in reverse gear and back off at high speed.
    b. quickly jump overboard and push your boat into deeper water.
    c. check the condition of your hull.
    d. move all passengers to the forward deck and try to back off.

22. **When towing, never tie to an improperly mounted cleat. Cleats used for towing should always be:**
    a. screwed to the boat with long, heavy screws.
    b. both cemented and screwed to the boat.
    c. attached to the deck with strong water-proof glue.
    d. through-bolted with a backing block.

23. **If a person falls overboard, one of your first actions should be to:**
    a. stop the boat and immediately set off a visual distress flare.
    b. stop forward motion and back up quickly to retrieve the person from the water.
    c. shout "Man Overboard" so that your helmsman hears you.
    d. approach from the direction of the wind and current, come close by, and toss the victim a line.

24. **When encountering restricted visibility of any kind, your first reaction should be to:**
    a. reduce speed so you will be able to stop in one-half the distance you can see.
    b. put on foul weather gear to keep from getting cold and wet.
    c. ring your ship's bell one short ring every second to advise other vessels of your presence.
    d. use your hailer every three minutes to announce that you are underway and ask all other vessels to keep clear.

25. **If your boat swamps or capsizes, the primary rule to remember is:**
    a. immediately send someone over the side to swim for help.
    b. always stay with the boat.
    c. swim some distance from the boat to avoid oil slicks.
    d. fasten a line to the boat and ask all to help pull it ashore.

26. **If involved in a collision your first action is to:**
    a. get the name, address, and insurance company of the operator of the other boat.
    b. check your VHF radio to see if it is damaged.
    c. place fenders between the two boats to eliminate further damage.
    d. account for and check the condition of your crew and the occupants of the other boat.

Boat Smart

27. If fire breaks out on your boat, immed-ately notify your crew, have them put on life preservers, and:
    a. empty the contents of your fire extinguisher in the general area of the flame.
    b. instruct your crew to move to the unaffected portion of the boat.
    c. stay with the boat, even if the fire cannot be extinguished.
    d. turn the boat so that the wind will fan the fire and help put it out.

28. Hypothermia is:
    a. excessive perspiration and thirst resulting from exposure to the sun for a long period of time.
    b. the abnormal lowering of the body's internal temperature due to exposure to cold air, wind, or water.
    c. a hallucinating reaction resulting from excessive loss of moisture in brain tissue.
    d. an abnormal raising of the body's internal temperature due to exposure to warm air, wind, or water.

29. Carbon monoxide poisoning is most frequently caused by exposure to:
    a. fumes from an overloaded holding tank.
    b. oil vapors emitted from a crankcase ventilation valve.
    c. exhaust from engines, generators, cabin heaters, and galley stoves.
    d. fumes from stale bait deteriorating in the bait well.

30. The use of a marine radiotelephone on a recreational boat is restricted to:
    a. distress, safety, operational, and public correspondence communications on permitted channels.
    b. trivial chatter on channels 68, 69, 70, 71, 72, 78.
    c. calling the Coast Guard on Ch 68 for a radio check.
    d. obtaining weather broadcasts on channels 24, 25, 26, 27, 28, 84, 85, 86, 87, 88.

31. An emergency distress signal on Channel 16 requesting urgent assistance for a vessel threatened with immediate danger to life or property is a _____ emergency call.
    a. Security
    b. Mayday
    c. Help
    d. Pan-Pan

32. Calling channels for recreational vessels to contact other vessels or shore stations are:
    a. 8 & 7.
    b. 11& 9.
    c. 16 & 9.
    d. 17 &14.

33. The following type of call is a felony and incurs stiff penalties:
    a. a Security call.
    b. request for a radio check.
    c. hoax Mayday call.
    d. Pan-Pan call.

U.S. AIDS TO NAVIGATION SYSTEM
on navigable waters except Western Rivers

LATERAL SYSTEM AS SEEN ENTERING FROM SEAWARD

PORT SIDE ODD NUMBERED AIDS	PREFERRED CHANNEL NO NUMBERS-MAY BE LETTERED	PREFERRED CHANNEL NO NUMBERS-MAY BE LETTERED	STARBOARD SIDE EVEN NUMBERED AIDS

PORT SIDE ODD NUMBERED AIDS

■ GREEN LIGHT ONLY
- FLASHING (2)
- FLASHING
- OCCULTING
- QUICK FLASHING
- ISO

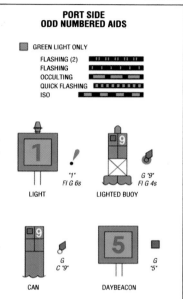

LIGHT — "1" Fl G 6s
LIGHTED BUOY — G "9" Fl G 4s
CAN — G C "9"
DAYBEACON — G "5"

PREFERRED CHANNEL NO NUMBERS-MAY BE LETTERED

PREFERRED CHANNEL TO STARBOARD TOPMOST BAND GREEN

■ GREEN LIGHT ONLY

COMPOSITE GROUP FLASHING (2+1)

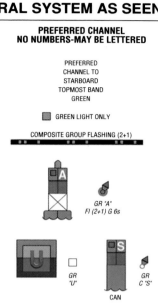

GR "A" Fl (2+1) G 6s
GR "U"
GR C "S"
CAN

PREFERRED CHANNEL NO NUMBERS-MAY BE LETTERED

PREFERRED CHANNEL TO PORT TOPMOST BAND RED

■ RED LIGHT ONLY

COMPOSITE GROUP FLASHING (2+1)

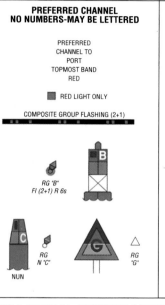

RG "B" Fl (2+1) R 6s
RG N "C"
RG "G"
NUN

STARBOARD SIDE EVEN NUMBERED AIDS

■ RED LIGHT ONLY
- FLASHING (2)
- FLASHING
- OCCULTING
- QUICK FLASHING
- ISO

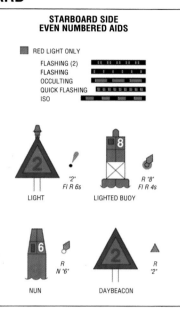

LIGHT — "2" Fl R 6s
LIGHTED BUOY — R "8" Fl R 4s
NUN — R N "6"
DAYBEACON — R "2"

AIDS TO NAVIGATION HAVING NO LATERAL SIGNIFICANCE

ISOLATED DANGER NO NUMBERS--MAY BE LETTERED

□ WHITE LIGHT ONLY

Fl (2) 5s

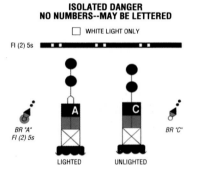

BR "A" Fl (2) 5s
BR "C"
LIGHTED
UNLIGHTED

SAFE WATER NO NUMBERS--MAY BE LETTERED

□ WHITE LIGHT ONLY   MORSE CODE

Mo (A)

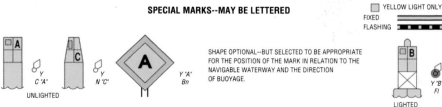

RW "N" Mo (A)
LIGHTED AND/OR SOUND
MR — RW "A"
SPERICAL — RW SP "B"
RW "N"
UNLIGHTED AND/OR SOUND

RANGE DAYBOARDS--MAY BE LETTERED

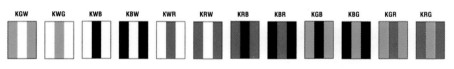

KGW KWG KWB KBW KWR KRW KRB KBR KGB KBG KGR KRG

DAYBOARDS--MAY BE LETTERED

□ WHITE LIGHT ONLY

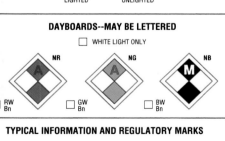

NR — RW Bn
NG — GW Bn
NB — BW Bn

SPECIAL MARKS--MAY BE LETTERED

□ YELLOW LIGHT ONLY
- FIXED
- FLASHING

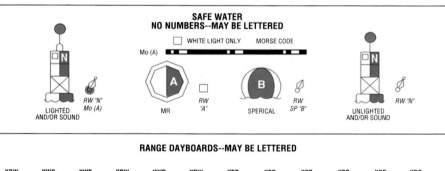

Y C "A"
Y N "C"
UNLIGHTED
Y "A" Bn
SHAPE OPTIONAL--BUT SELECTED TO BE APPROPRIATE FOR THE POSITION OF THE MARK IN RELATION TO THE NAVIGABLE WATERWAY AND THE DIRECTION OF BUOYAGE.
Y "B" Fl
LIGHTED

TYPICAL INFORMATION AND REGULATORY MARKS

INFORMATION AND REGULATORY MARKERS

WHEN LIGHTED, INFORMATION AND REGULATORY MARKS MAY DISPLAY ANY LIGHT RHYTHM EXCEPT QUICK FLASHING AND FLASHING (2)

□ WHITE LIGHT ONLY

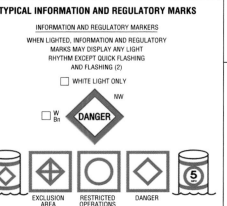

W Bn
DANGER NW
EXCLUSION AREA
RESTRICTED OPERATIONS
DANGER

Aids to navigation marking the Intracoastal Waterway (ICW) display unique yellow symbols to distinguish them from aids marking other waters. Yellow triangles △ indicate aids should be passed by keeping them on the starboard (right) hand of the vessel. Yellow squares ▢ indicate aids should be passed by keeping them on the port (left) hand of the vessel. A yellow horizontal band provides no lateral information, but simply identifies aids as marking the ICW.

Plate 1

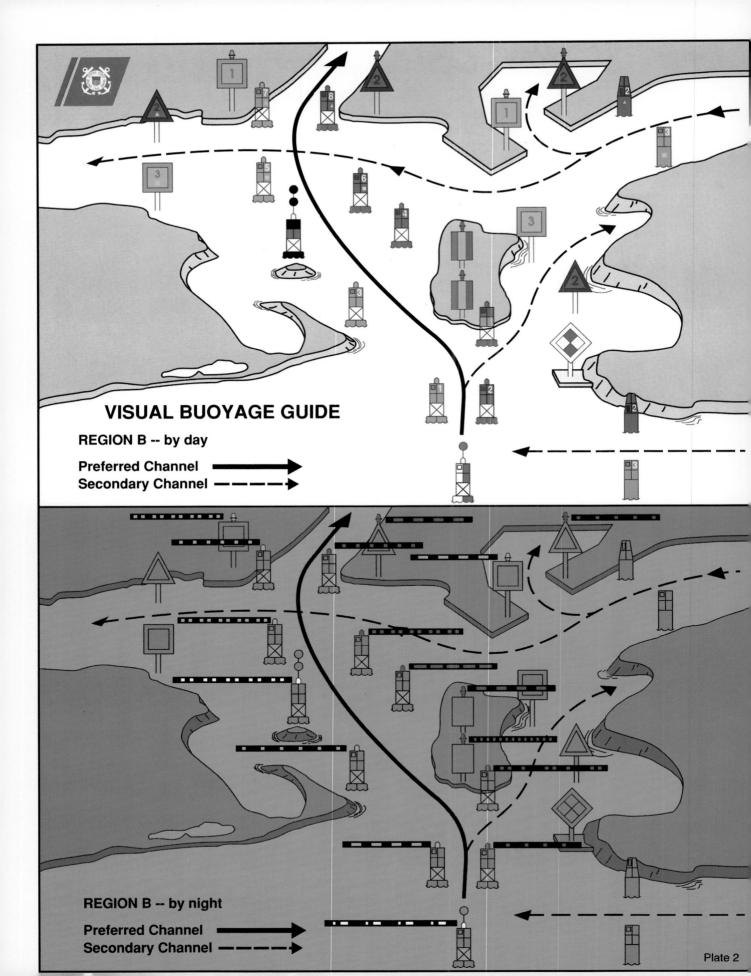

VISUAL BUOYAGE GUIDE

REGION B -- by day

Preferred Channel ⟶

Secondary Channel ⤏

REGION B -- by night

Preferred Channel ⟶

Secondary Channel ⤏

Plate 2

FICTITIOUS NAUTICAL CHART

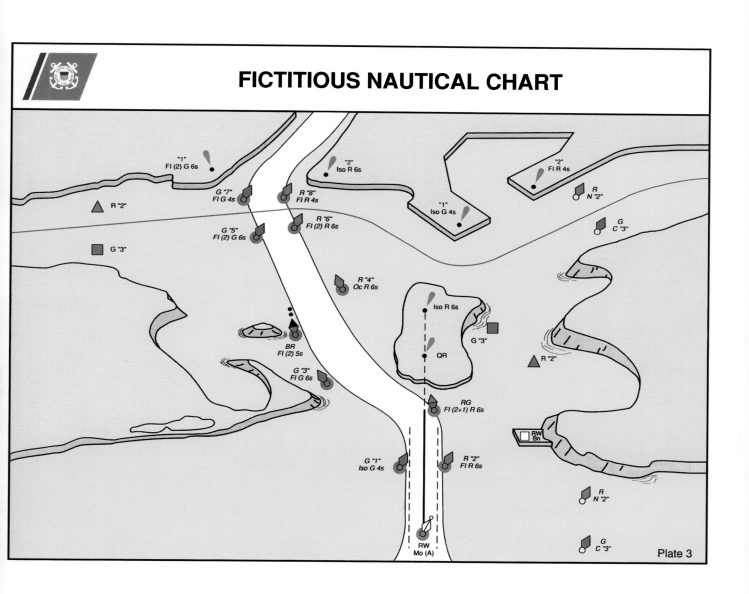

"1"
Fl (2) G 6s

"2"
Iso R 6s

"2"
Fl R 4s

G "7"
Fl G 4s

R "8"
Fl R 4s

R
N "2"

R "2"

"1"
Iso G 4s

G "5"
Fl (2) G 6s

R "6"
Fl (2) R 6s

G
C "3"

G "3"

R "4"
Oc R 6s

Iso R 6s

G "3"

BR
Fl (2) 5s

QR

R "2"

G "3"
Fl G 6s

RG
Fl (2+1) R 6s

RW
Bn

G "1"
Iso G 4s

R "2"
Fl R 6s

R
N "2"

RW
Mo (A)

G
C "3"

Plate 3

U.S. AIDS TO NAVIGATION SYSTEM
on the Western River System

AS SEEN ENTERING FROM SEAWARD

PORT SIDE
OR RIGHT DESCENDING BANK

☐ GREEN OR ☐ WHITE LIGHTS

FLASHING
ISO

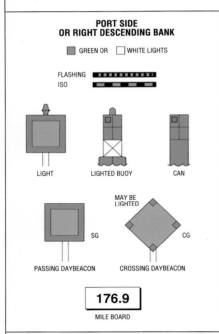

LIGHT   LIGHTED BUOY   CAN

MAY BE
LIGHTED

SG   CG

PASSING DAYBEACON   CROSSING DAYBEACON

176.9
MILE BOARD

PREFERRED CHANNEL

MARK JUNCTIONS AND OBSTRUCTIONS
COMPOSITE GROUP FLASHING (2 + 1)

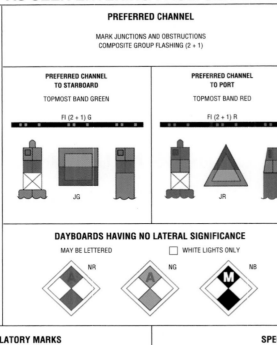

PREFERRED CHANNEL TO STARBOARD	PREFERRED CHANNEL TO PORT
TOPMOST BAND GREEN	TOPMOST BAND RED
Fl (2 + 1) G	Fl (2 + 1) R
JG	JR

DAYBOARDS HAVING NO LATERAL SIGNIFICANCE

MAY BE LETTERED   ☐ WHITE LIGHTS ONLY

 NR   NG   NB

STARBOARD SIDE
OR LEFT DESCENDING BANK

☐ RED OR ☐ WHITE LIGHTS

FLASHING (2)
ISO

LIGHT   LIGHTED BUOY   NUN

MAY BE
LIGHTED

TR   CR

PASSING DAYBEACON   CROSSING DAYBEACON

123.5
MILE BOARD

TYPICAL INFORMATION AND REGULATORY MARKS

INFORMATION AND REGULATORY MARKERS
WHEN LIGHTED, INFORMATION AND REGULATORY
MARKS MAY DISPLAY ANY LIGHT
RHYTHM EXCEPT QUICK FLASHING
AND FLASHING (2)

NW ☐ WHITE LIGHT ONLY

DANGER

EXCLUSION
AREA

RESTRICTED
OPERATIONS

DANGER

SPECIAL MARKS--MAY BE LETTERED

SHAPE: OPTIONAL--BUT SELECTED TO BE APPROPRIATE
FOR THE POSITION OF THE MARK IN RELATION TO THE
NAVIGABLE WATERWAY AND THE DIRECITON
OF BUOYAGE.

☐ YELLOW LIGHT ONLY

FIXED
FLASHING
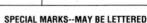

 A   C   NY A   B

UNLIGHTED   LIGHTED

UNIFORM STATE WATERWAY MARKING SYSTEM

STATE WATERS AND DESIGNATED STATE WATERS FOR PRIVATE AIDS TO NAVIGATION

REGULATORY MARKERS

BOAT
EXCLUSION
AREA

SWIM   AREA

ROCK — DANGER

SLOW
NO   WAKE

CONTROLLED
AREA

EXPLANATION MAY BE PLACED
OUTSIDE THE CROSSED DIAMOND
SHAPE, SUCH AS DAM, RAPIDS,
SWIM AREA, ETC.

THE NATURE OF DANGER MAY BE
INDICATED INSIDE THE DIAMOND
SHAPE, SUCH AS ROCK, WRECK,
SHOAL, DAM, ETC.

TYPE OF CONTROL IS INDICATED IN
THE CIRCLE, SUCH AS SLOW,
NO WAKE, ANCHORING, ETC.

MULLET LAKE
BLACK RIVER

INFORMATION

FOR DISPLAYING INFORMATION
SUCH AS DIRECTIONS, DISTANCES,
LOCATIONS, ETC.

BUOY USED TO DISPLAY
REGULATORY MARKERS

 5 MPH

MAY SHOW WHITE LIGHT
MAY BE LETTERED

LATERAL SYSTEM

MAY SHOW GREEN
REFLECTOR OR LIGHT

MAY SHOW RED
REFLECTOR OR LIGHT

USUALLY FOUND IN PAIRS
PASS BETWEEN THESE BUOYS

3   PORT SIDE ——— LOOKING UPSTREAM ——— STARBOARD SIDE   4

SOLID BLACK BUOY   SOLID RED BUOY

CARDINAL SYSTEM

MAY SHOW WHITE REFLECTOR OR LIGHT

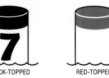

RED-STRIPED
WHITE BUOY

7

BLACK-TOPPED
WHITE BUOY

RED-TOPPED
WHITE BUOY

MAY BE LETTERED
DO NOT PASS BETWEEN
BUOY AND NEAREST SHORE

MAY BE NUMBERED

PASS TO NORTH
OR EAST OF BUOY

PASS TO SOUTH
OR WEST OF BUOY

MOORING
BUOY

WHITE WITH BLUE BAND

MAY SHOW WHITE
REFLECTOR OR LIGHT

Plate 4

A

Glossary

This is a glossary of terms used in this manual. A detailed glossary of nautical terms is available from USPS.

adrift–Unattached to shore or bottom, floating out of control.

aft, after–At, near, or toward the stern.

aground–Touching or stuck on the bottom.

ahead–1. The direction toward the bow of a boat (relative to the position of the observer); 2. In front of a boat; 3. Moving in a forward direction. (Compare astern.)

Aids to Navigation–Charted objects available to assist in determination of position or safe course or to warn of danger (e.g., buoys, beacons, fog signals, lights, radio beacons, range marks). Also, any electronic device used for navigation.

amidships–In or near the middle of the boat.

anchor–Device used to secure boat to bottom of body of water.

astern–1. The direction toward the stern of the boat (relative to the position of the observer). 2. In back of or behind a boat; 2. Moving in reverse (backwards). (Compare ahead.)

athwartship–Direction at right angles to the centerline of a boat.

auxiliary–The engine of a sailboat; a sailboat with an auxiliary engine.

back–1. Change in direction of the wind in a counter-clockwise direction in the Northern Hemisphere, and a clockwise direction in the Southern Hemisphere (See Veer.); 2. To cause to move backwards.

backfire–Ignition of the fuel-air mixture in the intake manifold by a flame from a cylinder. Usually caused by a too-lean mixture in a gasoline-fueled engine. The opposite of blasting.

backstay–Part of standing rigging, usually cable, that supports a mast from aft.

batten–1. A thin, narrow strip of wood, plastic, or fiberglass used to stiffen the leech of a sail; 2. A wooden strip fastened over a seam to stop leakage.

beacon–1. Anything that serves as a signal or indication for guidance or warning; 2. A fixed (non-floating) aid to navigation.

beam–1. Maximum width of a boat; 2. A horizontal athwartship support for the deck.

berth–1. A place to sleep a boat; 2. A boat's position at a pier or float; 3. A margin of safety as in "give it a wide berth."

bilge–Lowest part of a boat's interior.

blasting–Ignition of a too-rich fuel-air mixture in the exhaust system of an engine. Often confused with backfire.

boat hook–A pole with a hook on one end used to retrieve lines or other items. Also used to fend-off.

boom–Spar used to extend and control foot of fore-and-aft sail.

bow–Forward end of a boat. (Compare stern.)

bow Line–A line used at the bow of a boat.

bridle–A length of line or wire rope with both ends secure (or a secured loop) to the middle of which another line is attached.

broach–Turn a boat broadside to wind or waves, subjecting it to possible capsizing.

buoy–Anchored floating device used as an aid to navigation. May carry a light, horn, whistle, bell, gong, or combination for identification. Also may be used to mark a mooring (i.e., anchor buoy).

buoyancy–The upward force exerted by a fluid on a body or object in that fluid. The upward force that keeps a boat floating.

cabin–The enclosed or decked-over living space of a boat.

capsize–To turn over, upset.

cast off–Let go a line; set loose, unfasten; undo all mooring lines in preparation for departure.

catamaran–Boat with twin, narrow hulls connected by a deck or crossbeams, resulting in a wide beam and good stability.

centerboard–Pivoted board that can be lowered through a slot in the keel to reduce leeway.

chafing gear–Sacrificial wrapping around lines, rigging, or spars to prevent wear.

chain plate–Metal strap on a sailboat, usually secured to the hull or bulkhead or elsewhere, to which a shroud or stay is attached.

channel–Portion of a waterway that is navigable, usually marked and having a known depth of water.

chart–A map intended primarily for navigational use by aircraft or vessels.

chock–1. Fitting to guide a line or cable: 2. Wedge or block to keep an object from moving.

cleat–Fitting, usually with two projecting horns, to which lines are made fast.

cleat hitch–A figure-eight hitch used to attach a line to a cleat.

cockpit–Well or sunken space in the deck.

COLREGS–International Regulations for Preventing Collisions at Sea, included as the International Rules in the Navigation Rules published by the United States Coast Guard and distributed by the Government Printing Office. These Rules are applicable on waters outside of established navigational lines of demarcation. The lines are called COLREGS Demarcation Lines and delineate those waters upon which mariners shall comply with the Inland and International Rules.

compass error–Combined effect of variation and deviation.

crest–The top of a wave.

cuddy–A shelter cabin in a small boat.

current–1. The horizontal movement of water; 2. The movement of electrons on a conductor.

Daybeacon, Daymark–Unlighted fixed aid to navigation.

daysailer–Sailboat without amenities, such as a cabin, used for short duration sailing or racing.

dead reckoning (DR)–Calculating a boat's position based on its course, speed, and time run from a previous position.

deck–The portion of the boat covering the hull.

deck house–A partially enclosed structure erected on the deck.

deviation (D, Dev)–Disturbing effect of a boat's magnetic field upon its compass. Numerical difference in degrees, measured east (E) or west (W), between the magnetic value and the compass value of a given direction.

dinghy–Small open boat used as a lifeboat or tender.

displacement–The weight of water displaced by a floating vessel; hence, the weight of the vessel itself.

dock–1. Area of water, within which a vessel can be made fast, between two landing piers or wharves; 2. To guide a vessel alongside a float, pier, or wharf.

draft–1. Depth of water needed to float a boat; 2. The fullness or "belly" of a sail.

drift–1. Movement of a boat due to wind and current; 2. Velocity (speed) of current.

drogue–Drag deployed off the stern of a boat to create resistance and slow the boat's speed in heavy weather, but still allow steerageway. Often conical or series of conical shapes. (See sea anchor.)

fairway–A channel.

fender–Protective device between a boat and another object.

fiberglass–A glass fiber material usually impregnated with a synthetic resin such as polyester or epoxy; may be woven (mat) or random fibers.

flame arrestor–A screen-like metal fitting fastened over a carburetor air intake to keep backfire flames from flashing out of an air intake into an engine compartment where they could ignite gasoline fumes.

Float Plan–An outline plan of a cruise left at one's home port or with friends to provide a description of the boat, list of persons on board, list of safety equipment carried, and, most importantly, where the boat will be cruising and when it is expected to return to home port.

flybridge (flying bridge)–A steering position located atop the cabin of a powerboat.

fore–Denoting at, near, or towards the bow.

foredeck–The deck of a boat located near the bow.

forestay–A stay below and aft of the headstay on a sailboat. (see Headstay).

forward–Toward the bow. (Compare aft.)

foul–Jammed, entangled; not clear; being hindered or impeded.

freeboard–Vertical distance from the water surface to the lowest point where unwanted water could come aboard.

galley–1. Area where food is stored and cooked; 2. A nautical kitchen.

gear–1. General name for all non-permanent nautical equipment, including crew's clothing and personal effects; 2. A toothed wheel that interlocks with another toothed wheel to transmit motion (transmission gears).

Give-way Vessel–A term from the Navigation Rules, used to describe the vessel that must yield in meeting, crossing, or overtaking situations. Compare Stand-on Vessel

Global Positioning System (GPS)–A satellite-based world-wide navigation system using simultaneous signals from three or more satellites to establish highly accurate positioning.

gunwale–Upper edge or rail of a boat. (Pronounced "gun'el.")

halyard–Line for hoisting sails or flags.

hatch–Closable opening in the deck.

head–1. Marine toilet and its compartment; 2. Upper corner of a triangular sail or upper edge of a four-sided sail; 3. Upper end of mast, masthead; 4. Foremost part of boat, bow.

heading–Direction in which a boat is pointing at a given moment.

headsail–Any sail flown forward of the mast.

headstay–A stay running from the top of a mast to the bow or bowsprit and is the outermost stay on boats with more than one headsail; a jibstay.

heel–Incline to one side due to force of wind or waves.

helm–The tiller or wheel and related steering gear.

helmsman–The person steering the boat with the tiller or wheel.

hitch–A knot used to secure a rope fast to another rope or other object.

hull–Basic structure and shell of a boat.

inboard–Toward the centerline of the boat; inside the boat.

inboard/outboard (I/O)–Propulsion system with an inboard engine connected through the transom to an outboard drive unit (see Stern Drive).

jib–Triangular sail set on a stay forward of the mast.

jibstay–The forwardmost stay supporting the mast, extending from the bow or bowsprit to the upper part of the mast.

keel–Main centerline structural member (backbone) of a boat. Also, downward extension of hull to increase lateral resistance and stability.

knot–1. General term for securing a line to an object, another line, or itself; 2. Unit of speed of one nautical mile per hour.

latitude–Angular distance on the earth's surface, measured north and south of the earth's equator.

launch–1. To place a boat in the water; 2. A boat used to carry people between shore and a moored vessel.

leeway–1. Sideways movement of a boat through the water caused by wind; 2. The angular difference due to wind between the true course steered and the true course over the ground.

life jacket–A buoyant vest called Personal Flotation Device (PFD) in the United States.

life preserver–A buoyant coat, suit, vest, ring, horseshoe buoy, or cushion called Personal Flotation Device (PFD) in the United States.

longitude–Angular distance on the earth's surface east or west of the prime meridian (000°) extending north and south through Greenwich, England

mainsail–Boat's principal sail, set aft of mainmast (pronounced "mains'el").

marina–A facility for berthing recreational boats.

mark–Any object required by sailing instructions to be passed by a boat on a specific side.

mast–1. A vertical spar on a sailboat on which sails may be set; 2. A vertical spar on a powerboat from which may be flown a steadying sail or flags or burgees (may be used with a boom to lift gear).

Mayday–The term used to signify an urgent distress communication under international radiotelephone procedures; the highest priority transmission, indicating there is immediate danger to a vessel or to someone onboard.

nautical mile–A unit of distance equal to one minute of latitude and equal to approximately 6,076.1 feet or 1.15 statute miles.

Navigation Rules–The Rules of the Road of the United States, governing navigation lights, rules for vessels meeting or passing, sound signals, and distress signals.

outboard–Toward the outside of a boat.

outboard motor–An engine with propeller attached, designed to be fastened to the transom of a boat.

Pan-Pan–The term used to signify an urgent communication under international radiotelephone procedures; the second highest priority transmission, indicating that the safety of the vessel or someone onboard is involved, but the need for assistance is not immediate (pronounced "pahn-pahn").

pay out–Slacken or let out a line gradually.

pendant–Short rope serving as an extension of a line, chain, or cable with descriptive name based on use; e. g., mooring pendant (usually pronounced "pen'ant").

Personal Floatation Device (PFD)–A buoyant coat, suit, vest, ring, horseshoe buoy, or cushion.

Personal Watercraft (PWC)–Class-A boat using an inboard engine to drive a water jet pump for motive power, designed to be operated by a person sitting, standing, or kneeling on the vessel.

pier–Structure extending into the water from shoreline to provide dockage.

pile–A pole or post driven vertically into the bottom, usually to support a pier or float or to moor a boat.

piling–A structure of piles often used to protect wharves and piers.

piloting–A means of navigating using reference points that may be seen or determined from information on charts—such as depths, heights or ranges.

planing hull–A hull designed to climb towards the surface of the water as sufficient power is applied and to skim along the water at a greatly reduced displacement attitude.

port–1. Left side of a boat when facing the bow; 2. Toward the boat's left; 3. Opening in a boat's side (e. g., portlight or port hole); 4. A harbor.

quarter–1. After part of a boat's side, (e.g., port quarter); 2. Direction 45 degrees abaft the beam.

raft–A floating platform.

rafting Up–Tying a group of boats together for a social gathering using only a few anchors.

range–1. Two or more objects in line;. 2. Maximum distance at which an object may be seen; 3. Distance between two points, such as a radar range to a navigational aid; 4. Difference in elevation (height) between any successive pair of high and low tides.

rig–1. To prepare a boat for sailing; 2. Arrangement of spars and sails (e.g., as on a sloop).

rigging–All the lines and gear used to support the spars and control the sails.

rode–Anchor line and/or chain.

rudder–A flat board, blade, or plate hung on the aft end of a boat and used to steer the boat.

rudder post–The shaft to which a rudder blade is attached. The tiller or other steering apparatus is affixed to the other end.

running rigging–The lines used to raise, set, and trim the sails.

scope–Ratio of the length of the payed out anchor line (rode) to the height of the chock above the bottom of the body of water.

screw–In nautical usage, an alternate name for the propeller.

sea anchor–A parachute-like or cone-shaped device deployed off the bow to hold a boat head-to-wind with minimum sternway; often used in heavy weather to keep the bow into the wind and seas. (Compare drogue.)

seaworthy–Said of a boat that is in fit condition to put to sea.

Sec-ur-ity–The international radio telephone procedural word for a message concerning the safety of navigation. Third in priority after Mayday and Pan-Pan. (Pronounced "say-cure-it-tay.")

shaft–A cylindrical rod. A rotating shaft that transmits power from the engine to the propeller.

sheet–Line used to adjust a sail relative to the wind (e.g., a jibsheet is used to adjust a jib).

shroud–Rigging, generally wire or rods, used to support a mast laterally.

snub–To stop a line from running out by taking a turn around a bitt or cleat.

sole–The floor of a cockpit or interior cabin.

spar–Any shaft or pole for the attachment of a sail, such as the mast, boom, yard, or sprit.

speed–Rate of motion.

spinnaker–A large, lightweight headsail set forward of the headstay and used when reaching or running. Spinnakers can be symmetrical or asymmetrical.

spring line–A line leading forward or aft from a vessel to a piling or fitting on a pier that prevents the boat from moving ahead or astern.

stability–The ability of a boat to resist heeling and overturning.

Stand-On Vessel–A term, from the Navigation Rules, used to describe the vessel that continues its course in the same direction and at the same speed during a crossing or overtaking situation, unless a collision appears imminent. (Compare Give-way Vessel.)

standing rigging–The permanent wires or rods, as well as associated parts, supporting the mast.

starboard–Side of a boat, or direction, to the right when facing toward the bow.

stay–Standing rigging used to support a mast fore and aft.

stem–The upright structural member or post of the bow, attached to the foremost part of a vessel's keel.

stern–After end of a boat.(Compare bow.)

stern drive–An inboard/outboard drive system with the engine inside the boat (see Inboard/Outboard).

stern line–A mooring line that runs from the aft end of a boat to a float, a piling or a pier.

stow–To put something in its proper place.

strand–1. To drive a vessel ashore or aground. 2. One of the lays of a rope (the wound yarns or fibers that are woven with other strands to make a rope).

superstructure–Cabins, deckhouses, etc. above the deck.

tender–1. A small boat accompanying a vessel, used to transport persons, gear, and supplies, a dinghy. 2. A lower than average resistance to heeling.

thunderstorm–A storm produced by a cumulonimbus cloud. The thunderstorm is accompanied by lightning and thunder, usually with strong gusts, heavy rain, and sometimes hail.

tidal range–Difference in height of tide between any successive pair of high and low tides.

tide–The vertical rise and fall of ocean water (most noticeable in coastal regions) resulting mainly from the gravitational attraction of the moon and sun.

tiller–A lever attached to the upper end of a rudder post, used by the helmsman to turn the rudder.

topside–On or above the weather deck (wholly exposed to the elements).

topsides–The sides of a vessel between the water line and the deck.

transom–The portion of the hull at the stern that is at right angles to the centerline of the boat.

trim–1. To adjust the set of the sail; 2. Refers to the attitude of a boat at rest in the water.

trimaran–A boat with three hulls connected by a deck or crossbeams, resulting in a wide beam and good stability; the middle hull is usually larger than the outer hulls.

trip line–1. A buoyed line attached to the crown of an anchor for the purpose of freeing it when fouled; 2. A line fastened to the small end of the cone of a sea anchor to collapse it, thus spilling the water from the cone.

turnbuckle–A tension-adjusting device for tightening wire rigging or cable, composed of threaded rods inside a threaded barrel.

variation (V, Var)–The angle between the geographic meridian and the magnetic meridian at a given locality. Variation is easterly (E) or westerly (W), as the direction of the magnetic meridian is toward the east or west of geographic north.

veer–1. Change in direction of the wind in a clockwise direction in the Northern Hemisphere and a counter- clockwise direction in the Southern Hemisphere (See Back); 2. To change direction or course.

wake–Water surface turbulence left by a moving boat.

way–Movement of a vessel through the water, such as headway, sternway, or leeway.

winch–A geared drum turned by a handle and used to pull lines such as sheets and halyards.

WX channels(s)–Weather broadcast channels, usually considered to be those available on a marine VHF radiotelephone.

B

Navigation Light Requirements

Powerboats

Light requirements on power-driven vessels depend upon the length of the vessel, with some permissible options:

- Option 1) Under International and Inland Rules, the sidelights of a vessel under 65.6 ft (20m) in length may be combined into one lantern carried on the fore and aft centerline of the vessel.
- Option 2) Both Inland and International Rules allow a power-driven vessel less than 39.4 feet (12 m) to exhibit an all-round white light and sidelights, in place of masthead light, stern light, and sidelights.

- Option 3) Under International Rules only, a vessel less than 23 feet (7 m) with a maximum speed of less than 7 knots, may exhibit an all-round white light in place of masthead and sternlights. It should display sidelights, if practicable.

Powerboats Underway				
Vessel Length	White Masthead Light Forward	Sidelights Red & Green	White Sternlight	Options
Less than 39.4 ft (12meters)	Needed (2nd optional)	Needed	Needed	1–2–3 Below
Greater than 39.4 ft, but less than 65.6 ft (20meters)	Needed (2nd optional)	Needed	Needed	1 Below
Greater than 65.6 ft, but less than 164 ft (50meters)	Needed (2nd optional)	Needed	Needed	
Greater than 164 ft (50meters)	2 needed, 1 aft of & higher than the forward.	Needed	Needed	

Sailboats

2 Sailboats under both sail and power must exhibit the lights of a power driven vessel, as described on page 115. However, during daylight hours, International Rules require a sailboat under both sail and power to display a black conical day shape, pointed end down. This is not *required* under Inland Rules, if the boat is less than 39.4 feet (12 meters), although the shape *may* be used.

Sailboats Underway

3 Light requirements for sailing vessels *not* under auxiliary power depend upon the length of the vessel. They do *not* display a masthead light. Their sidelight and sternlight requirements are the same as for a powerboat of the same size.

- Option 1) The sidelights of a vessel under 65.6 ft (20m) in length may be combined into one lantern carried on the fore and aft centerline of the vessel.

- Option 2) A sailing vessel under 65.6 feet (20 m) may combine sidelights and sternlight into one lantern carried near or at the top of the mast. This tri-color light is recommended for vessels sailed offshore, because it will be more easily seen. It *must not* be used when under power.

- Option 3) A sailing vessel underway, in addition to sidelights and sternlight, may exhibit at or near the top of the mast, an all-round red light over an all-round green light. (These lights *may not* be used with the combination lantern option.)

- Option 4) If it is not practicable for sailing vessels under 23 feet (7 meters) to exhibit sidelights and sternlights, they may carry an electric torch or lantern showing a white light to be displayed in time to prevent collision.

Navigation Light Visibility Requirements

The required visibility of vessel lights depends on the length of the vessel. Larger vessels have different requirements than those shown.

Sailboats Underway			
Vessel Length	Sidelights Red/Green	White Sternlight	Options *
Less than 23 ft (7m)	Needed	Needed	1, 2, 3, 4
Greater than 23 ft. (7m), but less than 65.6 ft (20m)	Needed	Needed	1, 2, 3
Greater than 65.6 ft (20m)	Needed	Needed	3
*As stated in Column 1 (to left).			

Navigation Light Visibility Requirements		
	Vessel Length	
Light	Less than 39.4 ft	Greater than 39.4 ft, but less than 65.6 ft (20m)
White Masthead Light	2 miles	3 miles
Green & Red Sidelights	1 mile	2 miles
White Sternlight	2 miles	2 miles
All-Round Lights	2 miles	2 miles

C

State Boating Law Agencies

This is a list of agencies where you can obtain material regarding the boating laws for your area. In many states, this document is free. There may be a local source for this information: County Sheriff's Office, Marine Laws Enforcement Office, or Natural Resources office.

The list includes websites which are frequently subject to change.

ALABAMA (AL)
Dept. of Conservation & Natural Res, Marine Police Div
64 N. Union St, Rm 438
Montgomery, AL 36130-3020
Tel.: 334-353-2628
Web: www.dcnr.state.al.us

ALASKA (AK)
Dept. of Natural Resources,
Div Parks and Outdoor Recreation
Office of Boating Safety
550 W. 7th St., Ste 1370
Anchorage, AK 99501-3561
Web: www.alaskaboatingsafety.org

ARIZONA (AZ)
Arizona Game & Fish Dept.
Law Enforcement
2221 W. Greenway Rd
Phoenix, AZ 85023
Tel.: 602-789-3381
Web: www.azgfd.com

ARKANSAS (AR)
Arkansas Game & Fish Comm.
Boating Administration
#2 Natural Resources Dr.
Little Rock, AR 72205
Tel.: 501-223-6495
Web: www.agfc.state.ar.us

CALIFORNIA (CA)
Dept. of Boating & Waterways
2000 Evergreen St
Sacramento, CA 95815-3888
Tel.: 916-263-8181
Web: www.dbw.ca.gov

COLORADO (CO)
Dept. of Natural Resources
Div. Parks & Outdoor Rec
13787 S. Hwy 85
Littleton, CO 80125
Phone: 303-791-1954
Web: http://parks.state.co.us/boating/

CONNECTICUT (CT)
Dept. of Environmental Protection
Boating Div.
333 Ferry Rd
POB 280 Old Lyme, CT 06371-0280
Phone: 860-434-8638
Web: www.dep.state.ct.us

DELAWARE (DE)
Dept. of Natural Resources & Environmental Control
Div. Fish & Wildlife Enforcement
89 Kings Hwy
Dover, DE 19901
Tel.: 302-739-3440
Web: www.dnrec.state.de.us/fw/fwwel

DISTRICT OF COLUMBIA (DC)
Metro Police Dept.
Harbor Patrol Sect
550 Water Street, SW
Washington, DC 20024
Tel.: 202-727-4582
Web: www.mpdc.dc.gov

FLORIDA (FL)
Fish & Wildlife Conservation Comm
620 S. Meridian St
Tallahassee, FL 32399-1600
Tel.: 850-488-5600, Ext 178
Web: www.floridaconservation.org

GEORGIA (GA)
Dept. of Natural Resources
Wildlife Resources Div
Law Enforcement Section
2070 US Hwy 278, SE
Social Circle, GA 30025
Tel.: 770-784-3068
Web: www.dnr.state.ga.us

HAWAII (HI)
Dept. of Land & Natural Resources
Div Boating & Ocean Recreation
333 Queen St, Ste 300
Honolulu, HI 96813
Tel.: 808-587-3250
Web: www.state.hi.us/dlnr/dbor/dbor

IDAHO (ID)
Dept. of Parks & Recreation
Boating Program
POB 83720
Boise, ID 83720-0065
Tel.: 208-334-4180 ext. 227
Web: www.idahoparks.org

ILLINOIS (IL)
Dept. of Natural Resources
Ofc Law Enforcement
One Natural Resources Way
Springfield, IL 62702-1271
Tel.: 217-785-7742
Web: www.dnr.state.il.us

INDIANA (IN)
Dept. of Natural Resources
Law Enforcement Div
402 W. Washington St., Rm W255-D
Indianapolis, IN 46204
Tel.: 317-232-4010
Web: www.state.in.us/dnr

IOWA (IA)
Dept. of Natural Resources
Conservation and Recreation Div.
Wallace State Ofc Bldg
East Ninth & Grand Ave.
Des Moines, IA 50319-0034
Tel.: 515-281-8652
Web: www.state.io.us/dnr

KANSAS (KS)
Dept. of Wildlife & Parks
1020 S. Kansas Ave., Rm 200
Topeka, KS 66612
Tel.: 785-296-2281
Web: www.kdwp.state.ks.us

KENTUCKY (KY)
Div Law Enforcement
Dept. of Fish & Wildlife
Tourism Cabinet
#1 Game Farm Rd
Frankfort, KY 40601
Tel.: 502-564-3176
Web: www.kdfwr.state.ky.us

LOUISIANA (LA)
Dept. of Wildlife & Fisheries
Enforcement Div
POB 98000
Baton Rouge, LA 70898-9000
Tel.: 225-765-2984
Web: www.wlf.state.la.us

MAINE (Inland) **(ME)**
Dept. of Inland Fisheries & Wildlife
284 State St
Augusta, ME 04333
Tel.: 207-287-5220
Web: www.mefishwildlife.com

MAINE (Marine) **(ME)**
Dept. of Marine Resources
State House Sta. #21
Augusta, ME 04333-0021
Tel.: 207-624-6555
Web: www.maine.gov/dmr

MARYLAND MD)
Dept. of Natural Resources
Natural Resources Police
Tawes State Office Bldg E-3
580 Taylor Ave.
Annapolis, MD 21401
Tel.: 410-260-3280
Web: www.dnr.state.md.us

MASSACHUSETTS
Dept. of Fisheries, Wildlife & Environmental Law Enforcement
Div. Law Enforcement
251 Causeway St, Ste 400
Boston, MA 02114
Tel.: 617-727-8760
Web: www.mass,gov/dfwele/dle

MICHIGAN (MI)
Dept. of Natural Resources
Law Enforcement Div
P.O. Box 30031
Lansing, MI 48909
Tel.: 517-335-3422
Web: www.dnr.state.mi.us

MINNESOTA (MN)
Dept. of Natural Resources
500 Lafayette Rd
St. Paul, MN 55155-4046
Tel.: 651-296-0895
Web: www.dnr.state.mn.us

MISSISSIPPI (MS)
Dept. of Wildlife, Fisheries & Parks
Law Enforcement Div
1505 Eastover Dr
Jackson, MS 39211
Tel.: 601-432-2070
Web: www.mdwfp.com

MISSOURI (MO)
Dept. of Public Safety
Missouri State Water Patrol
POB 1368
Jefferson City, MO 65102-1368
Tel.: 573-751-3333
Web: www.mswp.state.mo.us

MONTANA (MT)
Montana Fish, Wildlife & Parks
Law Enforcement Div
1420 E. Sixth Ave.
Helena, MT 59620
Tel.: 406-444-2615
Web: www.fwp.state.mt.us

NEBRASKA (NE)
Nebraska Game & Parks Comm
Outdoor Education Div
2200 N 33rd St
Lincoln, NE 68503-0370
Tel.: 402-471-5579
Web: www.ngpc.state.ne.us/boating

NEVADA (NV)
Div of Wildlife
Law Enforcement Bureau
1100 Valley Rd
Reno, NV 89512-2817
Tel.: 775-688-1548
Web: http://nevadadivisionofwildlife.org

NEW HAMPSHIRE (NH)
NH Dept. of Safety
Div Safety Svcs
31 Dock Rd
Gilford, NH 03246-7627
Tel.: 888-254-2125
Web: www.state.nh.us/safety/dss

NEW JERSEY (NJ)
New Jersey State Police
Marine Services Unit
POB 7068
West Trenton, NJ 08628-0068
Tel.: 609-882-2000, Ext. 6173
Web: www.state.nj.us/njsp.org

NEW MEXICO (NM)
Energy, Minerals & Natural
Resources Dept.
State Parks Div
Boating Safety Sect
P.O. Box 1147
Sante Fe, NM 87505
Tel.: 505-744-5998
Web:www.emnrd.state.nm.us
/nmparks/

NEW YORK (NY)
Ofc Parks, Rec & Historic Pres
Bureau Marine & Rec Vehicles
Agency Bldg #1, 13th Floor
Empire State Plaza
Albany, NY 12238-0001
Tel.: 518-474-0445
Web: www.nysparks.com/boats

NORTH CAROLINA (NC)
Wildlife Resources Comm
Div of Enforcement
1717 Mail Service Ctr
Raleigh, NC 27699-1717
Tel.: 919-733-7191
Web: www.ncwildlife.org

NORTH DAKOTA (ND)
Game & Fish Dept.
Conserv & Comm Div
100 N Bismarck Expy
Bismarck, ND 59501-5095
Tel.: 701-328-6312
Web: www.state.nd.us/gnf/

OHIO (OH)
Dept. of Natural Resources
Div of Watercraft
4435 Fountain Sq Dr, Bldg A
Columbus, OH 43224-1300
Tel.: 614-265-6504
Web:www.dnr.state.oh.us/odnr
/watercraft

OKLAHOMA (OK)
Oklahoma Highway Patrol
Lake Patrol Sect
POB 11415
Oklahoma City, OK 73136-0415
Tel.: 405-425-2363
Web: www.dps.state.ok.us

OREGON (OR)
Oregon State Marine Board
435 Commercial St, NE, #400
POB 14145
Salem, OR 97309-5065
Tel.: 503-373-1405, Ext. 241
Web: www.boatoregon.com

PENNSYLVANIA (PA)
Pennsylvania Fish & Boat Comm
POB 67000
Harrisburg, PA 17106-7000
Tel.: 717-705-7849
Web: www.fish.state.pa.us

PUERTO RICO (PR)
Dept. of Env & Nat Resources
Commissioner of Navigation
POB 9066600
Plaza De Tierra Station
San Juan, PR 00906-6600
Tel.: 787-724-2340

RHODE ISLAND (RI)
Dept. of Environmental Manage-
ment
83 Park St
Providence, RI 02903
Tel.: 401-222-2284
Web: www.state.ri.us/dem.htm

SOUTH CAROLINA (SC)
Dept. of Natural Resources
Marine Law Enf/Educ Affairs
POB 12559
Charleston, SC 29422-2953-9378
Web: www.dnr.state.sc.us

SOUTH DAKOTA (SD)
Dept. of Game, Fish & Parks
Div of Wildlife
523 E. Capital
Pierre, SD 57501-3182
Tel.: 605-773-4506
Web: www.state.sd.us/gfp/

TENNESSEE (TN)
Tennessee Wildlife Resources Agcy
Boating Div
POB 40747
Nashville, TN 37204
Tel.: 615-781-6601
Web: www.state.tn.us/twra

TEXAS (TX)
Parks & Wildlife Dept.
Law Enforcement Div
4200 Smith School Rd
Austin, TX 78744
Tel.: 512-389-4568
Web: www.tpwd.state.tx.us

UTAH (UT)
Division of Parks & Wildlife
1594 W. N. Temple, Ste 116
POB 146001
Salt Lake City, UT 84114-6001
Tel.: 801-538-7464
Web: www.stateparks.utah.gov

VERMONT (VT)
State Police
Recreational Enf & Educ Unit
2777 St. George Rd
Williston, VT 05495-7429
Tel.: 802-878-7111
Web: www.dsp.state.vt.us

U.S. VIRGIN ISLANDS (VI)
Dept. of Planning & Natural
Resources - Enforcement
Cyril E. King Airport, 2nd Fl
St. Thomas, VI 00802
Tel.: 340-774-3320, Ext 5186

VIRGINIA (VA)
Dept. of Game & Inland Fisheries
4010 W. Broad St
POB 11104
Richmond, VA 23230-1104
Tel.: 804-367-1125
Web: www.dgif.state.va.us

WASHINGTON (WA)
Washington State Parks & Recre-
ation Comm
Boating Programs
7219 Cleanwater Lane, Bldg 17
PO Box 2650
Olympia, WA 98504-2650
Tel.: 360-586-6599
Web: www.parks.wa.gov

WEST VIRGINIA (WV)
Div Natural Resources
Law Enforcement Sect
Capitol Complex, Bldg 3
Charleston, WV 25305
Tel.: 304-558-2783
Web: www.dnr.state.wv.us

WISCONSIN (WI)
Dept. of Natural Resources
Bureau of Law Enforcement
101 S. Webster St
PO Box 7291
Madison, WI 53707-7291
Tel.: 608-264-8970
Web:www.dnr.state.wi.us/org/es
/enforcement/safety/boatsaf.htm

WYOMING (WY)
Wyoming Game & Fish Dept.
5400 Bishop Blvd
Cheyenne, WY 82006-0001
Tel.: 307-777-4686
Web: www.gf.state.wy.us

D

United States Coast Guard District Offices

These are the United States Coast Guard District Offices and the contacts for boating safety at those offices for the various United States, Territories and Possessions.

1st Coast Guard District
Office of Search and Rescue
408 Atlantic Ave.
Boston, MA 02110-3350
Phone: 617-223-8464
Web: www.uscg.mil/d1
Connecticut, Maine, Massachusetts, New Hampshire, New York, Rhode Island, Vermont

5th Coast Guard District
Chief of Operations
431 Crawford St.
Portsmouth, VA 23704-5004
Phone: 757-398-6204
Web: www.uscg.mil/d5
Delaware, District of Columbia, Maryland, New Jersey, North Carolina, Pennsylvania, Virginia

7th Coast Guard District
Chief of Operations
909 SE First Ave.
Miami, FL 33131-3050
Phone: 305-415-7057
Web: www.uscg.mil/d7
Florida, Georgia, Puerto Rico, South Carolina, U.S. Virgin Islands

8th Coast Guard District
Chief, Recreational Boating Safety
501 Magazine St.
New Orleans, LA 70130-3396
Phone: 504-589-6770
Web: www.uscg.mil/d8
Alabama, Arkansas, Colorado, Illinois, Indiana, Iowa, Kansas, Kentucky, Louisiana, Mississippi, Missouri, Nebraska, New Mexico, North Dakota, Oklahoma, South Dakota, Tennessee, Texas West Virginia, Wyoming

9th Coast Guard District
Office of Law Enforcement
1240 E. 9th St.
Cleveland, OH 44199-2060
Phone: 216-902-6094
Web: www.uscg.mil/d9/d9boating /boatingsafety/html
Michigan, Minnesota, Ohio, Wisconsin

11th Coast Guard District
Chief of Operations
Building 51-1, Coast Guard Island
Alameda, CA 94501-5100
Phone: 510-437-5364

Web: www.uscg.mil/d11
Arizona, California, Nevada, Utah
13th Coast Guard District
Chief of Search & Rescue
915 Second Ave.
Seattle, WA 98174-1067
Phone: 206-220-7257
Web: www.uscg.mil/d13
Idaho, Montana, Oregon, Washington

14th Coast Guard District
Chief of Operations
300 Ala Moana Blvd., Rm 9-236
Honolulu, HI 96850
Phone: 800-818-8725, Option #5, or 808-541-2161
Web: www.uscg.mil/d14/
Hawaii, Guam, American Samoa, Northern Mariana Islands

17th Coast Guard District
Chief Maritime Operations
P.O. Box 25517
Juneau, AK 99802-5517
Phone: 907-463-2297
Web: www.uscg.mil/d17
Alaska

USPS FLOAT PLAN

Complete this form before going boating and leave it with a reliable person who can be depended upon to notify the Coast Guard or other rescue organization in case who do not return as scheduled. *Do not file this form with the Coast Guard.* A word of caution: In case you are delayed, and it is not an emergency, inform those with your float plan, the police and/or Coast Guard of your delay in order to avoid an unnecessary search.

1. Name of person filing this plan and telephone number _____

_____

2. Description of boat: Type_____Color_____

   Trim_____Registration number _____

   Length_____Name_____Make _____

3. Persons aboard — Name(s)   Age   Address & Telephone Number

   _____   ____   _____

   _____   ____   _____

   _____   ____   _____

   _____   ____   _____

   _____   ____   _____

   _____   ____   _____

4. Engine type_____ Horsepower _____

   Number of engines_____ Fuel capacity _____

5. Survival equipment (check as appropriate):

   ☐Life preservers ☐Flares ☐Signal mirror ☐Horn ☐Smoke signals ☐Flashlight ☐Raft or dinghy ☐EPIRB ☐Paddles ☐Food

   ☐Water ☐Anchor(s) ☐Cellular Telephone (Number) _____Other (Specify)_____

6. Radio: Yes / No   Type _____ Frequencies _____ Call sign _____

7. Trip expectations: Leaving from _____ Going to _____

   Leaving (Date) _____ (Time)_____ AM/PM.– Return by (Date)_____ Time _____ AM/PM

   But in no event later than (Date)_____ (Time)_____AM/PM

8. Other pertinent information _____

9. Vehicle: Make_____ Color _____ License Number _____

   Trailer license number_____ Where parked _____

10. If not returned by (Date)_____ (Time) _____ AM/PM call:

    U.S. Coast Guard, Tel. number_____

    or, Local Authority (Name)_____ Tel # _____

Distributed by
United States Power Squadrons – Sail and Power Boating
For information about Boating Classes in your area, call 1-800-336-2628

Boating Accident Report **Complete All Blocks** (If Not Applicable, Mark "NA")	Operators and owners of recreational boats must file a written report if an accident results in: a. Loss of life or disappearance from a vessel (report within 48 hours); b. An injury requiring medical treatment beyond first-aid (report within 10 days); or, c. Complete loss of the boat or property damage in excess of $2000 (report within 10 days). Submit your report to authorities in the State where the accident occurred. This form is provided to help you if you must file a report. Describe what happened (sequence of events). Include failure of equipment. Include a diagram if needed. Continue on additional sheets of paper if necessary. Include any information regarding the involvement of alcohol and/or drugs in causing or contributing to the accident. Include any descriptive information about the use of PFDs. (Use aditional sheets of paper if necessary.)

Accident Data

Date of Accident	Time AM PM	Name of Body of Water	Location (give location precisely)
Number of Vessels Involved	**Nearest City or Town**	**County**	**State**	**ZIP Code**

Weather (Check all that apply)
[ ] Clear   [ ] Rain
[ ] Cloudy   [ ] Snow
[ ] Fog   [ ] Haze

Water Conditions
[ ] Calm (Waves less than 6 in.)
[ ] Choppy (Waves 6 in. to 2 ft.)
[ ] Rough (Waves 2 to 6 ft.)
[ ] Very rough (Greater than 6 ft.)
[ ] Strong Current

Temperature (Estimated)
Air _____ °F

Water _____ °F

Wind (mph)
[ ] None
[ ] Light (0-6)
[ ] Moderate (7-14)
[ ] Strong (15-25)
[ ] Storm (Over 25)

Visibility
Day   Night
[ ] Good   [ ] Good
[ ] Fair   [ ] Fair
[ ] Poor   [ ] Poor

Name of Operator	**Operator Address**

Operator Telephone
(___) ____-_____

[ ] Male   [ ] Female

Date of Birth
Mo____ Day____ Yr____

Operator Experience
[ ] None
[ ] Under 100 hrs.
[ ] Over 100 hrs

Boating Safety Instruction
[ ] State Course
[ ] United States Power Squadrons
[ ] USCG Auxiliary
[ ] American Red Cross
[ ] None

Name of Owner	**Owner Address**

Owner Telephone
(___) ____-_____

Number of People Onboard

Number of People Being Towed

Rented Boat?
[ ] Yes   [ ] No

Boat No. 1 (Your Boat)

Boat Registration/Documentation Number	**State**	**Hull I.D. No.**	**Boat Name**
Boat Manufacturer	**Length**	**Model**	**Year Built**

Boat Type
[ ] Open Motorboat
[ ] Cabin Motorboat
[ ] Auxiliary Sail
[ ] Sail Only
[ ] Rowboat
[ ] Canoe/Kayak
[ ] Pontoon Boat
[ ] Houseboat
[ ] Other (Specify)

Hull Material
[ ] Wood
[ ] Aluminum
[ ] Steel
[ ] Fiberglass
[ ] Rubber/Vinyl/Canvas
[ ] Rigid Hull Inflatable
[ ] Other (Specify)
_____

Engine
[ ] Outboard
[ ] Inboard
[ ] I/O (Inboard/ Outboard Stern
[ ] Airboat

Fuel
[ ] Gasoline
[ ] Diesel
[ ] Electric

Propulsion
[ ] Propeller
[ ] Water Jet
[ ] Air Thrust
[ ] Manual
[ ] Sail

Number of Engines _____
Total Horsepower
_____

PFD's
Was boat adequately equipped with Coast Guard Approved PFDs?
[ ] Yes   [ ] No
Were PFDs Accessible?
[ ] Yes   [ ] No

Fire Extinguishers Onboard?
[ ] Yes   [ ] No
Used?
[ ] Yes   [ ] No

Information at Time of Accident

Operation (Check all that apply)
[ ] Cruising
[ ] Changing Direction
[ ] Changing Speed
[ ] Drifting
[ ] Towing
[ ] Being Towed
[ ] Rowing/Paddling
[ ] Sailing
[ ] Launching
[ ] Docking/Undocking
[ ] At Anchor
[ ] Tied to Dock/Moored
[ ] Other (Specify)

Activity (Check if any apply)
[ ] Fishing
[ ] Tournament
[ ] Hunting
[ ] Swimming/Diving
[ ] Making Repairs
[ ] Waterskiing/Tubing, etc.
[ ] Racing
[ ] Whitewater Sports
[ ] Fueling
[ ] Starting Engine
[ ] Non-recreational
[ ] Other (Specify)

Estimaed Speed (mph)
[ ] None
[ ] Less than 10
[ ] 10-20
[ ] 21-40
[ ] More than 40

Type
[ ] Grounding
[ ] Capsizing
[ ] Flooding/Swamping
[ ] Sinking
[ ] Fire or Explosion (Fuel)
[ ] Fire or Explosion (Other)
[ ] Skier Mishap
[ ] Collision with Other Vessel
[ ] Collision with Fixed Object
[ ] Collision with Floating Object
[ ] Fall Overboard
[ ] Fall in Boat
[ ] Struck by Boat
[ ] Struck by Motor/Propeller
[ ] Struck Submerged Object
[ ] Hit and Run
[ ] Other (Specify)

Contributing Factors? (Check if any apply)
[ ] Weather
[ ] Excessive Speed
[ ] Improper Lookout
[ ] Restricted Vision
[ ] Overloading
[ ] Improper Loading
[ ] Hazardous Waters
[ ] Alcohol Use
[ ] Drug Use
[ ] Hull Failure
[ ] Machinery Failure
[ ] Equipment Failure
[ ] Operator Inexperience
[ ] Operator Inattention
[ ] Congested Waters
[ ] Passenger/Skier Behavior
[ ] Dam/Lock
[ ] Other (Specify)

Injury (If more than two injuries, attach additional forms)

Name of Victim #1	Victim's Address	
Date of Birth	**Medical Aid Beyond First-Aid?** [ ] Yes [ ] No **Admitted to Hospital?** [ ] Yes [ ] No	**Describe Injury**
Was PFD Worn? [ ] Yes [ ] No **Inflatable?** [ ] Yes [ ] No	**Prior to Accident?** [ ] Yes [ ] No	**If No, as a Result of Accident?** [ ] Yes [ ] No

Name of Victim #2	Victim's Address	
Date of Birth	**Medical Aid Beyond First-Aid?** [ ] Yes [ ] No **Admitted to Hospital?** [ ] Yes [ ] No	**Describe Injury**
Was PFD Worn? [ ] Yes [ ] No **Inflatable?** [ ] Yes [ ] No	**Prior to Accident?** [ ] Yes [ ] No	**If No, as a Result of Accident?** [ ] Yes [ ] No

Death (If more than two fatalities, attach additional forms)

Name of Fatality #1	Victim's Address	**Was PFD Worn?** [ ] Yes [ ] No
Date of Birth: / / [ ] Male [[Female	**Death Caused by:** [ ] Drowning [ ] Other [} Disappearance	

Name of Fatality #2	Victim's Address	**Was PFD Worn?** [ ] Yes [ ] No
Date of Birth: / / [ ] Male [[Female	**Death Caused by:** [ ] Drowning [ ] Other [} Disappearance	

Other People Aboard Your Boat (If more than two other people, attach additional forms)

Name #1	Name #1 Address	
Date of Birth	**Was PFD Worn?** [ ] Yes [ ] No **If No, As a Result of Accident?** [ ] Yes [ ] No	**Prior to Accident?** [ ] Yes [ ] No **Was It Inflatable?** [ ] Yes [ ] No

Name #2	Name #2 Address	
Date of Birth	**Was PFD Worn?** [ ] Yes [ ] No **If No, As a Result of Accident?** [ ] Yes [ ] No	**Prior to Accident?** [ ] Yes [ ] No **Was It Inflatable?** [ ] Yes [ ] No

Boat #2 (If more than two vessels, attach additional forms)

Operator's Name	Operator's Address	
Operator's Telephone Number ( )	**Boat Registration/Documentation Number**	**State**
Owner's Name	**Owner's Address**	
Owner's Telephone Number ( )		

Property Damage

Estimated Amount $	Your Boat & Contents $	Other Boat(s) & Contents $	Other Property $

Describe Property Damage

Witnesses Not on Your Boat

Name	Address	Telephone Number ( )
Name	Address	Telephone Number ( )

Person Completing This Report

Name	Address	Telephone Number ( )
Signature	**Qualification** [ ] Operator [ ] Owner [ ] Investigator [ ] Other	**Date Submitted**

Accident Description (Use additional paper)

BOAT SMART℠ • Name _____ Date _____

You will learn much more from this Boat Smart course if you read each lesson and answer the review questions before the class discussion. Please turn in this answer sheet at the start of each class.

The sheet will be reviewed by a Proctor and returned to you at the break. If there is something you don't understand, please ask the Instructor or a Proctor for clarification.

1 • Getting Started

1. a b c d
2. a b c d
3. a b c d
4. a b c d
5. a b c d
6. a b c d
7. a b c d
8. a b c d
9. a b c d
10. a b c d
11. a b c d
12. a b c d
13. a b c d
14. a b c d
15. a b c d
16. a b c d
17. a b c d
18. a b c d
19. a b c d
20. a b c d
21. a b c d
22. a b c d
23. a b c d
24. a b c d
25. a b c d
26. a b c d
27. a b c d
28. a b c d
29. a b c d
30. a b c d
31. a b c d
32. a b c d
33. a b c d
34. a b c d
35. a b c d
36. a b c d

2 • What's Needed

1. a b c d
2. a b c d
3. a b c d
4. a b c d
5. a b c d
6. a b c d
7. a b c d
8. a b c d
9. a b c d
10. a b c d
11. a b c d
12. a b c d
13. a b c d
14. a b c d
15. a b c d
16. a b c d
17. a b c d
18. a b c d
19. a b c d
20. a b c d

3 • Rules to Live By

1. a b c d
2. a b c d
3. a b c d
4. a b c d
5. a b c d
6. a b c d
7. a b c d
8. a b c d
9. a b c d
10. a b c d
11. a b c d
12. a b c d
13. a b c d
14. a b c d
15. a b c d
16. a b c d
17. a b c d
18. a b c d
19. a b c d
20. a b c d
21. a b c d
22. a b c d
23. a b c d
24. a b c d
25. a b c d
26. a b c d
27. a b c d
28. a b c d
29. a b c d
30. a b c d
31. a b c d
32. a b c d
33. a b c d

We hope that Boat Smart is just the beginning of *your* boating education. While the course does give you valuable basics, that's just what they are—BASICS. Your local Power Squadron, as a unit of United States Power Squadrons (USPS®), offers a wide spectrum of courses to enhance your boating skills, safety, and enjoyment. It is truly the best boating education program in America. Ask any Squadron member for details about how you can join us to share in the many benefits of USPS membership. Remember—Safe boating is more fun.